SMART INSURANCE

Leveraging AI, Telematics, and Financial Data for Global Risk Solutions

Yagazie Patrick Anyanwu

Published in Nigeria By,

Prodigy Press

Contents

Preface

Insurance has always been about understanding risk. For centuries, insurers have used numbers, probabilities, and experience to predict what might go wrong and how to protect people against it. Yet, in the digital age, risk itself has become more dynamic. Data flows faster, decisions are made in real time, and the boundaries between technology, finance, and human behavior continue to blur. This transformation has created the foundation for what we now call smart insurance.

Smart insurance represents more than the digitalization of old systems. It embodies a complete rethinking of how data can be used responsibly to understand risk, prevent loss, and improve customer experience. Artificial intelligence, telematics, and financial analytics are at the core of this revolution. Each provides a different lens for observing and managing uncertainty, but together they create a connected, intelligent ecosystem. With the ability to collect, analyze, and interpret vast amounts of information, insurers can now respond to risk with unprecedented precision and fairness.

The goal of this book is to explore how modern technology is redefining the insurance landscape. It looks closely at the secure use of data within cloud environments, where most modern systems now operate. As organizations migrate from legacy databases to distributed infrastructures, questions of data security, compliance, and privacy have become central to the future of digital risk management. The integrity of telematics and financial data must be protected not only for ethical reasons but also to sustain public trust in the insurance ecosystem.

Another major focus of this book is the practical role of artificial intelligence and machine learning. These technologies are not theoretical concepts; they are now shaping underwriting, pricing, claims handling, and fraud detection across the world. Predictive models help insurers assess driver behavior and accident likelihood. Intelligent algorithms guide route optimization and vehicle maintenance planning. Even customer engagement and satisfaction are increasingly influenced by how effectively data-driven systems understand human patterns.

Throughout the chapters, readers will also encounter discussions about the relationship between financial data and decision-making. In the insurance business, profitability depends on accurate forecasting, consistent monitoring, and transparent communication. Dashboards and visualization tools have become indispensable in translating complex data into clear insights that executives, regulators, and analysts can act upon.

The ability to link telematics, financial metrics, and behavioral data in one coherent system is now a competitive advantage.

This book is not written only for technologists. It is intended for data science professionals, financial experts, business leaders, and graduate students who want to understand how digital intelligence is changing the insurance world. It provides both conceptual foundations and practical case studies drawn from global operations. Each chapter aims to make technical subjects accessible without losing analytical depth.

In creating this work, I was guided by a single question: how can we make insurance smarter, safer, and more inclusive in a data-driven world? The answer lies in collaboration between humans and machines, between technology and ethics, and between innovation and regulation. The insurance industry of the future will not be built by algorithms alone; it will be shaped by people who understand how to use those algorithms responsibly.

The journey of writing this book has reinforced my belief that the next generation of insurance professionals must think differently. They must see data as both a tool and a responsibility. They must design systems that protect privacy while delivering insight. And they must remember that behind every dataset is a human life, a story, and a need for security.

I invite you to explore these pages with an open mind. Whether you are a data scientist eager to apply your skills in a new industry, a policymaker shaping the future of digital regulation, or a student curious about how finance and technology intersect, this book is written with you in mind. Smart insurance is not a trend; it is the future of global risk solutions.

Foreword

The global insurance landscape is undergoing a transformation unlike anything witnessed before. What used to be a largely reactive industry, one that assessed damage and compensated losses after the fact has evolved into a proactive ecosystem built on intelligence, prediction, and prevention. The fusion of artificial intelligence, telematics, and advanced financial analytics has given rise to what we now recognize as smart insurance. It is no longer just about policies and premiums; it is about using data to understand risk in motion.

I have had the privilege of working with data scientists, financial analysts, and insurance executives across continents, and the shift is unmistakable. The world's leading insurers are no longer defined by their market share but by how effectively they use information. Those who master predictive technologies can anticipate claims before they happen, detect fraud in real time, and design personalized coverage that aligns with individual behavior. This ability to merge technology with insight has redefined competitiveness in the global risk market.

This book, *Smart Insurance: Leveraging AI, Telematics, and Financial Data for Global Risk Solutions,* arrives at a critical moment in this transformation. It serves as both a roadmap and a reflection of what is possible when technology meets responsibility. What makes this work stand out is its balance, it does not glorify data for its own sake, nor does it treat technology as a substitute for human judgment. Instead, it shows how artificial intelligence and secure data analysis can work together to create value while protecting trust.

Each chapter provides practical insights into how modern insurers are harnessing cloud computing, machine learning, and telematics data to enhance decision-making. The discussion of secure data handling is particularly relevant in an age when customer confidence depends on how well organizations safeguard information. The author's treatment of compliance, transparency, and ethics reminds us that technology must always serve people, not the other way around.

Perhaps the most compelling aspect of this book is how it brings theory to life through real-world applications. The exploration of predictive models for driver risk scoring, route optimization, and financial performance demonstrates that the smart insurance revolution is not confined to developed markets. Emerging economies are adopting these innovations rapidly, creating opportunities for inclusive growth and safer communities. The book also highlights how Nigerian and African professionals are contributing to this global dialogue, building data infrastructures, developing Insurtech startups, and participating in policy frameworks that shape the future.

As readers move through the chapters, they will find a recurring theme: the future of insurance belongs to those who can think across disciplines. Data scientists must understand finance; insurers must appreciate technology; and regulators must learn to adapt quickly to innovation. Collaboration across these fields is no longer optional, it is the foundation of modern risk management.

In the years ahead, we will see an even greater integration of quantum computing, blockchain, and decentralized risk modeling. Yet, the principles outlined in this book will remain constant: secure data, ethical intelligence, and measurable insight. These are the pillars upon which lasting innovation will stand.

This work is an invitation to professionals, students, and innovators alike to embrace the evolution of insurance with clarity and courage. It challenges us to see beyond disruption and recognize the opportunity in transformation. More importantly, it reminds us that every algorithm, dataset, and prediction ultimately serves one purpose to protect lives, assets, and livelihoods.

I commend the author for producing a book that speaks to both the technical and human sides of the insurance industry. It is a valuable contribution to the growing body of knowledge on how artificial intelligence and data science can make the world not only smarter but safer.

Introduction

Insurance has long been the quiet stabilizer of economies, a safety net for individuals and organizations facing the unpredictable turns of life and business. Yet beneath its formal structures and complex models lies a simple premise: understanding and managing risk. For centuries, this understanding was based on probability tables, historical loss patterns, and the intuition of experienced actuaries. But the digital era has completely rewritten that equation. We now live in an age where every second generates data, from vehicles transmitting driving patterns to wearable devices recording health indicators, from financial transactions painting behavioral profiles to sensors monitoring the weather. This new data ecosystem has redefined not only how risk is perceived but also how it is predicted, prevented, and priced. The insurance industry, once reactive and document-heavy, has become intelligent, data-centric, and adaptive to real-time conditions. This shift marks the birth of what we now call smart insurance.

Smart insurance is not an abstract concept but a living system powered by artificial intelligence, telematics, and financial analytics. It represents the fusion of technology and insight where data no longer sleeps in spreadsheets or archives but flows continuously through secure cloud systems, feeding models that learn, evolve, and respond to human behavior. Through AI and machine learning, insurers are no longer limited to post-incident compensation; they can now anticipate risks before they occur. A car that brakes too suddenly, a policyholder who drives aggressively at night, or a company that exhibits unusual transaction trends can all be flagged by predictive algorithms in real time. This intelligence transforms how insurance works, turning static contracts into dynamic relationships. Risk is no longer defined by what has happened in the past but by what is likely to happen next.

At the core of this transformation lies data; vast, complex, and continuous. Telematics, in particular, has introduced a new dimension to risk evaluation. Every modern vehicle, smartphone, and connected device acts as a sensor, capturing behavioral information that reflects real-world habits. The data tells stories: how fast someone accelerates, how they respond to obstacles, how consistently they maintain safe distances, and how their choices vary across routes and conditions. For insurers, this means the ability to personalize pricing and coverage in ways never possible before. Drivers with safer habits pay lower premiums, and fleets that adopt predictive maintenance practices reduce downtime and liability. Insurance, once driven by averages, is now driven by behavior. But with this opportunity comes great responsibility. The more data insurers collect, the more they must protect.

Secure data analysis is therefore the foundation of smart insurance. Modern insurers no longer store their information in isolated local servers but in scalable, cloud-based infrastructures that connect thousands of systems across the globe. These environments handle sensitive telematics and financial data that must remain confidential, intact, and compliant with international regulations. A single breach can undermine years of credibility. To prevent that, organizations are investing heavily in encryption, anonymization, and multi-layered access controls. Secure cloud computing allows distributed teams to analyze data collaboratively while ensuring that privacy and compliance remain uncompromised. It ensures that the power of artificial intelligence does not come at the cost of ethical integrity. In the age of digital insurance, security is not an afterthought; it is the system's backbone.

Artificial intelligence has also become the industry's most transformative engine. Beyond mere automation, AI brings foresight, the ability to simulate outcomes, recognize anomalies, and optimize decision-making. Through machine learning models, insurers can detect fraudulent activities by identifying patterns that humans might overlook. They can assess risks dynamically, adapting policies to changing behaviors, locations, and market conditions. Neural networks trained on large-scale accident data can predict frequency and severity, enabling companies to allocate resources more efficiently and price products more accurately. Even claims management, once considered a slow and human-intensive process, is being redefined by AI-driven assessment tools that can evaluate damage from photos or estimate repair costs instantly. The integration of AI into telematics and financial systems turns information into strategy and uncertainty into opportunity.

But the real revolution happens when these technologies merge. Imagine a single ecosystem where telematics feeds data into cloud analytics, where AI models interpret that data in real time, and where dashboards translate those insights into financial decisions. That ecosystem already exists in leading global insurers. Decision-makers now rely on live dashboards that display metrics such as claim ratios, loss frequencies, risk clusters, and customer churn probabilities. These visualizations help executives understand not only what has happened but also what is likely to happen next. Financial data analytics provides the quantitative bridge between predictive modeling and strategic planning. It helps insurers identify profitable segments, optimize capital distribution, and maintain liquidity while navigating volatile global markets. In this system, data is not an accessory, it is the currency of survival.

The evolution of smart insurance is not confined to advanced economies. Emerging markets, particularly in Africa and Asia, are embracing this transformation with remarkable speed. In Nigeria, for example, telematics-enabled mobile insurance platforms are reaching rural drivers who were once excluded from formal coverage. By leveraging cloud-based AI and behavioral scoring, local insurers are offering affordable premiums while reducing risk exposure. In Kenya, data-driven microinsurance models are protecting farmers against climate-induced losses. These innovations demonstrate that smart insurance is not a luxury for developed nations but a necessity for global financial inclusion. The ability to analyze data securely and act on insights quickly is what will define competitiveness in the decades ahead.

However, the path forward is not without complexity. With great intelligence comes greater ethical responsibility. The question is not only what we can do with data, but what we should do with it. Artificial intelligence must be governed by frameworks that protect fairness, transparency, and accountability. Telematics systems must collect only the data necessary for risk analysis, and financial decision-making must avoid biases that disadvantage vulnerable groups. Regulators and policymakers around the world are grappling with these challenges, seeking to create rules that balance innovation with protection. The insurance industry sits at the center of this balance, trusted to handle some of the most personal and sensitive data while driving technological progress that benefits society.

The purpose of this book is to explore these intersections; between technology and trust, automation and ethics, data and decision-making. It is written for data scientists, financial professionals, insurance executives, and graduate students who want to understand not just how smart insurance works, but why it matters. It brings together technical concepts, real-world applications, and emerging research to illustrate how AI, telematics, and financial analytics can work in harmony to create global risk solutions. Each chapter builds upon the last, guiding readers through the core principles of data security, predictive modeling, financial analysis, and intelligent system design. Together, these topics form a blueprint for the future of insurance, one that is smarter, safer, and more sustainable.

As the digital age accelerates, the boundaries between industries will continue to dissolve. Insurers will collaborate with data scientists, software engineers, policymakers, and behavioral economists to shape the next generation of intelligent systems. The convergence of AI and finance will make risk prediction more accurate, while telematics will ensure that those predictions are grounded in real human behavior. Financial data analytics will continue to translate this intelligence into strategic action, driving profitability and resilience. The result will be a world where insurance is no longer viewed as a reactive safety net but as a proactive partner in everyday life.

In this new reality, success will depend not only on how much data insurers possess, but on how responsibly they use it. The challenge is to build a future where innovation and integrity move together, where technology protects rather than exploits, and where every data point serves a purpose larger than profit. Smart insurance is more than an evolution of systems, it is a reimagination of trust in the age of information. And that trust will determine how the next era of global risk management is written.

Chapter 1 UNDERSTANDING THE FOUNDATIONS OF SMART INSURANCE

Insurance has always reflected how society understands risk. In every era, the tools and ideas used to manage uncertainty have evolved alongside technology and human behavior. The merchants of ancient Babylon and China developed early methods of sharing loss among traders, ensuring that no single voyage could destroy a merchant's livelihood. By the seventeenth century, actuarial science and probability transformed this practice into a formal discipline. For many generations, insurance remained a business of predictions drawn from experience. Policies were priced according to historical averages, while claims were processed manually by experts who relied on limited data. This traditional approach served its time, but as the modern world became faster, more complex, and more interconnected, the limits of this model began to show. Global commerce, digital communication, and technological dependency produced new types of risk that could no longer be understood through the old methods.

The twenty-first century brought with it a revolution driven by data. Every second now produces vast streams of information from digital devices, sensors, and transactions. Insurance companies discovered that these data streams could reveal patterns of behavior in real time rather than waiting for historical evidence. The result was the birth of what professionals now call smart insurance, a model that uses artificial intelligence, telematics, and financial analytics to make sense of continuous data. Instead of relying on estimates and assumptions, insurers can now study actual patterns of driving, spending, or environmental change and adjust their policies accordingly. Smart insurance represents a shift from reaction to prediction and from assumption to observation.

Artificial intelligence lies at the heart of this transformation. Through algorithms that can learn from large amounts of data, AI allows insurers to move beyond the limits of traditional statistics. Machine learning models analyze thousands of factors at once, finding relationships that human analysts would never notice. For example, a system can study years of driving data to predict accident probabilities or detect fraudulent claims by comparing new reports with hidden patterns in older ones. AI is not simply faster than manual processing; it is adaptive. With every new dataset, it refines its understanding of how risk behaves, improving the precision of pricing, claims management, and fraud prevention.

Telematics adds another layer of intelligence by linking behavior directly to data. A telematics device in a car can record acceleration, speed, braking, and route information. These measurements are transmitted securely to cloud systems, where they are analyzed by AI models. This continuous feedback loop allows insurers to offer personalized pricing, rewarding careful drivers and helping customers improve their habits. Similar systems exist in health insurance, where wearable devices track physical activity, heart rate, and sleep patterns. These innovations have redefined fairness in insurance. Instead of assigning risk based on broad demographic categories like age or gender, insurers can now calculate it based on verified behavior.

However, the expansion of telematics and AI also introduces new responsibilities. Data is no longer a static record stored in a filing cabinet. It is a living asset that must be protected, encrypted, and governed with absolute integrity. The success of smart insurance depends on secure cloud environments that guarantee confidentiality and compliance with international data protection laws. Encryption, identity management, and real-time monitoring have become as essential to insurers as underwriting and claims processing once were. Data security is not only a technical requirement; it is the foundation of public trust. Customers must know that their personal and financial information is protected from misuse or unauthorized access.

The cloud infrastructure that powers modern insurance enables global collaboration and scalability. Instead of local servers limited by storage capacity, cloud systems allow companies to analyze information from multiple regions simultaneously. This distributed architecture reduces risk by eliminating single points of failure. It also allows insurers to adapt quickly to regulatory changes or sudden market shifts. But the cloud must be used wisely. A poorly managed system can expose sensitive data and damage reputations. The new era of smart insurance demands that technical innovation and governance progress together.

Financial data plays an equally important role in shaping this evolution. Beyond customer information and behavioral insights, insurers depend on financial analytics to manage capital, forecast trends, and assess profitability. AI-driven models help organizations predict claims frequency, allocate reserves efficiently, and balance growth against solvency requirements. Executives and regulators rely on dashboards that visualize key performance indicators such as loss ratios, retention rates, and premium growth. These tools turn abstract data into clear insights that can guide strategic decisions. A well-designed dashboard can reveal inefficiencies, highlight opportunities, and even forecast systemic risks that could affect entire markets.

The real value of smart insurance lies in how these elements work together. Artificial intelligence transforms raw data into insight. Telematics captures real-world behavior. Financial analytics translates that insight into strategy. Combined, they create a feedback system that continuously learns and adapts. This system not only improves business performance but also encourages safer choices among customers. Drivers who know they are being scored based on behavior tend to drive more responsibly. Companies that monitor their operational data reduce waste and improve safety. Smart insurance is therefore not just an innovation in business models but a catalyst for behavioral change and societal improvement.

In emerging markets, this transformation has special significance. Many people in developing countries have historically lacked access to formal insurance because traditional models required extensive paperwork and credit histories. Smart insurance removes these barriers. Mobile telematics, digital payments, and cloud analytics allow insurers to reach customers who were previously excluded. In Nigeria, for example, startups now provide affordable motor and health insurance through mobile platforms that use AI to analyze driving or lifestyle data. These systems create inclusion by replacing credit-based assessments with data-based evidence. They also stimulate economic growth by giving individuals and small businesses the confidence to take productive risks.

Despite its benefits, smart insurance faces several challenges. Legacy infrastructure, fragmented data systems, and a shortage of skilled professionals can slow adoption. Many insurers operate with old databases that cannot easily integrate with new technologies. Others struggle with the ethical and legal implications of collecting continuous behavioral data. Cybersecurity threats also remain a serious concern. A single breach can compromise millions of records and erode public confidence. Addressing these challenges requires both investment and cooperation among industry players, regulators, and researchers. Standardized data formats, open interfaces, and strong privacy frameworks will be crucial to ensuring that innovation does not outpace accountability.

The transition from traditional to smart insurance represents more than a technological shift; it is a philosophical one. The goal is not only to process claims faster or calculate premiums more accurately but to prevent losses altogether. This shift moves insurance from a safety net to a predictive partner in people's lives. Vehicles, homes, and even personal health will be monitored in real time to prevent damage before it happens. This approach promises to make insurance not only more efficient but also more humane.

To understand the foundation of smart insurance is to understand that technology and trust must evolve together. Artificial intelligence can make systems intelligent, but only ethics and transparency can make them credible. Telematics can provide data, but only security can make that data meaningful. Financial analytics can reveal patterns, but only human judgment can interpret them wisely. The future of insurance will depend on how well these elements are balanced. The companies that succeed will be those that combine innovation with integrity and intelligence with empathy.

Smart insurance is therefore not the replacement of human expertise with machines, but the amplification of human capability through technology. It represents a new social contract between insurers and the insured, one grounded in mutual understanding, responsibility, and foresight. As the following chapters will show, this contract is reshaping global industries, influencing regulation, and redefining how we measure risk in a world that never stops moving.

1.1 Education and the New Knowledge Economy in Insurance

The growth of smart insurance is reshaping not only how policies are written but also how professionals are trained. Traditional insurance education focused heavily on mathematics, law, and finance. While these remain essential, they are no longer sufficient on their own. The new landscape demands literacy in data analytics, artificial intelligence, cybersecurity, and digital ethics. Professionals must understand not just how to read actuarial tables but how to interpret complex datasets produced by connected devices and machine learning systems.

Universities and professional institutions are beginning to adjust. Courses in actuarial science now include modules on Python programming, data visualization, and statistical learning. Graduate programs in finance and business analytics are incorporating telematics and risk informatics into their curricula. This convergence between academia and industry signals a deeper transformation. Insurance is no longer an isolated sector; it is part of the global knowledge economy where technology and data define competitive advantage.

In developing regions, this transformation holds enormous potential for capacity building. Partnerships between insurers, universities, and government agencies can create ecosystems where innovation thrives. For instance, research collaborations can produce local solutions to data challenges such as irregular internet access, unreliable reporting systems, or lack of standardized records. By developing indigenous talent skilled in both technology and policy, countries can position themselves as leaders in data-driven risk management. The ability to interpret complex insurance data will soon become as valuable a skill as underwriting or financial modeling once was.

Continuous learning will also become a cultural necessity within organizations. Smart insurance companies will invest in upskilling programs that teach their employees how to interact with AI tools and understand digital ethics. Leaders will need to balance automation with empathy, data analysis with judgment, and innovation with prudence. The human capacity to adapt and learn will remain the most reliable form of intelligence in the industry.

1.2 Sustainability and the Future of Risk Intelligence

Another area gaining momentum in the foundations of smart insurance is sustainability. Climate change, energy transition, and environmental volatility have created a new generation of risks that cannot be understood through historical patterns alone. Floods, droughts, and extreme temperatures are now more frequent and less predictable. To respond effectively, insurers are turning to AI-based climate models, satellite telematics, and geospatial analytics. These tools help predict environmental hazards and assess their impact on assets, crops, and infrastructure.

Sustainable insurance goes beyond responding to environmental loss. It also encourages responsible behavior among clients. Companies can use data analytics to design incentives for low-carbon operations, renewable energy investments, and safer logistics practices. Vehicle telematics can measure emissions and reward eco-friendly driving habits. Agricultural insurance can use satellite imagery to support farmers who adopt climate-smart practices. In this sense, smart insurance contributes to the global sustainability agenda by turning data into accountability.

Financial data also plays a critical role in sustainability. Insurers that analyze their investment portfolios can identify exposure to high-risk or environmentally damaging industries. By redirecting capital toward green bonds, clean energy projects, and socially responsible enterprises, they help shape a more resilient global economy. The power of data allows insurers to quantify their impact and communicate it transparently to regulators and investors.

The next frontier of smart insurance will combine environmental intelligence with social and governance analytics. Predictive models will evaluate not only physical risks but also reputational and ethical factors. Insurance will no longer protect only against property or casualty loss but also against failures in sustainability performance. This approach will require collaboration among scientists, data analysts, and policymakers to build risk frameworks that reflect the realities of a changing planet.

In this emerging vision, smart insurance becomes more than a financial product. It becomes a force for global stability, guiding decisions that affect economies, communities, and ecosystems. As climate data, telematics, and financial analytics converge, insurers will gain a deeper understanding of how human behavior interacts with natural systems. The companies that embrace this responsibility will not only survive but lead. Their success will depend on how well they can align profitability with sustainability, intelligence with conscience, and data with purpose.

Chapter 2 TELEMATICS AND THE DATA-DRIVEN ECOSYSTEM

Telematics has become one of the most influential forces shaping modern insurance. It represents the merger of telecommunications and informatics, allowing continuous transmission and analysis of data from vehicles, devices, and other connected systems. Through telematics, insurers no longer rely on assumptions or generalized statistics. They can now observe behavior, conditions, and performance in real time. This technology has turned data into a living resource, transforming the way risk is measured, priced, and managed.

The core principle of telematics is connection. Every second, vehicles equipped with sensors generate thousands of data points on speed, acceleration, braking, cornering, and location. This data is transmitted through mobile networks to secure cloud environments, where it is analyzed using artificial intelligence and machine learning. The result is a system that can evaluate driver behavior dynamically rather than retroactively. For insurers, this has changed everything. It is now possible to develop pricing models based on how a policyholder actually drives instead of relying on broad categories such as age, gender, or region. This personalization makes insurance fairer, more transparent, and more engaging for customers.

Telematics first found its application in the automobile industry. Early adopters included fleet managers who wanted to monitor vehicle usage and driver safety. Over time, insurers recognized its potential for underwriting. Usage-based insurance models, commonly referred to as UBI, emerged as a direct outcome of this realization. Under a UBI policy, premiums are calculated based on mileage, driving behavior, or specific conditions rather than fixed estimates. The better one drives, the less one pays. This approach creates a feedback loop that rewards responsibility while reducing claim frequency.

The advantages of telematics go far beyond pricing. The same data that determines premiums can also prevent accidents. For instance, by analyzing patterns in braking and cornering, AI algorithms can identify drivers at higher risk of collision and send early warnings or tailored recommendations. Fleet operators can receive alerts when vehicles deviate from safe routes or exceed speed limits. Predictive maintenance systems can detect mechanical issues before they cause breakdowns. This integration of analytics into daily operations has turned telematics from a monitoring tool into a preventive system that saves lives and reduces losses.

Telematics also enables faster and more accurate claims processing. In the event of an accident, connected vehicles can automatically send impact data, location coordinates, and even dashcam footage to the insurer. This instant reporting eliminates lengthy disputes over fault and accelerates claim approval. Some advanced systems use algorithms to reconstruct the event, determining whether sudden deceleration or lateral impact indicates genuine damage. The accuracy of such data reduces fraud and enhances customer satisfaction by shortening resolution times.

In health and life insurance, telematics has taken a different form through wearable devices and mobile health applications. Fitness trackers and smartwatches now provide continuous data on steps taken, heart rate, sleep quality, and stress levels. Insurers use this information to encourage healthy lifestyles and reward positive behavior. Policyholders who meet activity targets or maintain healthy habits receive discounts or bonuses. This model promotes preventive healthcare while reducing long-term claim costs. It also strengthens engagement between insurers and clients, transforming what used to be a once-a-year transaction into an ongoing relationship built on shared goals.

In logistics and commercial insurance, telematics is invaluable. Global supply chains depend on timely deliveries and safe cargo management. Telematics systems track vehicles, ships, and containers in real time, providing updates on location, temperature, humidity, and vibration. These details are crucial for industries like pharmaceuticals or food distribution, where a small deviation can lead to massive losses. By combining sensor data with predictive analytics, insurers can estimate exposure levels and provide specialized coverage. Clients benefit from transparency, while insurers gain precise insight into operational risk.

However, the data-driven ecosystem of telematics is not without its complexities. The collection, transmission, and storage of massive amounts of data present challenges related to privacy, security, and governance. Every piece of information transmitted through a telematics system carries potential exposure. Unauthorized access, misuse, or leakage can damage customer trust and lead to regulatory penalties. Insurers must therefore design their systems with security at the core. Encryption, anonymization, and strict access controls are essential. Equally important is the ethical handling of data. Policyholders must understand what data is being collected, how it is used, and what benefits they receive in return. Transparency transforms surveillance into service.

In this new ecosystem, data quality is as important as data quantity. A system flooded with inaccurate or incomplete data produces unreliable insights. For this reason, insurers invest heavily in calibration, validation, and filtering processes to ensure integrity. Artificial intelligence models rely on clean and consistent data to perform effectively. A single error in measurement can distort predictions or bias decisions. The responsibility lies not only with insurers but with every stakeholder in the chain, from manufacturers of telematics devices to software developers and data analysts. Each must maintain standards that ensure accuracy and accountability.

Another critical element in the telematics revolution is interoperability. The insurance industry depends on collaboration across multiple technologies, vendors, and jurisdictions. Vehicles from different manufacturers use different sensor configurations and communication protocols. Insurers operating globally must manage data from diverse sources and formats. Without standardized systems, integration becomes slow and costly. The emergence of open APIs and shared data frameworks is solving this challenge. These interfaces allow data from different systems to flow seamlessly into centralized platforms for analysis. This interconnectedness not only improves operational efficiency but also supports innovation.

The success of telematics also depends on infrastructure. Reliable mobile networks, advanced cloud services, and real-time analytics engines are essential for performance. In regions where network coverage is inconsistent, data transmission may be delayed or incomplete. This creates challenges for accurate monitoring and risk prediction. Governments and private companies must collaborate to build stronger digital foundations. As 5G networks expand globally, the capacity to process telematics data will multiply, enabling faster, more responsive systems. Vehicles will communicate with one another and with road infrastructure in real time, creating entire ecosystems of shared intelligence.

Despite its promise, telematics faces cultural and regulatory resistance. Some drivers or businesses worry that constant monitoring invades privacy. Others fear that data could be used unfairly to penalize customers rather than reward them. Overcoming these concerns requires education and communication. Insurers must explain the purpose of telematics clearly and emphasize its benefits. When people understand that their data can lead to lower premiums, safer driving, and better service, acceptance increases. Regulation will also play a role in protecting fairness. Laws must define how long data can be stored, who can access it, and how it can be shared. Strong oversight ensures that technological progress remains aligned with public interest.

Telematics is not limited to road vehicles. Aviation, marine, agriculture, and property insurance are also exploring its possibilities. Aircraft and ships already use advanced sensors to monitor fuel efficiency, mechanical performance, and weather conditions. Agricultural insurers use satellite imagery combined with on-ground sensors to assess soil quality and crop health. Real-time monitoring of buildings through smart devices can alert insurers to water leaks, electrical faults, or fire risks. The reach of telematics extends wherever data can be collected and transmitted. It is redefining risk not as a static possibility but as a dynamic event that can be observed and managed continuously.

The broader implication of this data-driven ecosystem is the creation of collective intelligence. As millions of devices send data simultaneously, patterns emerge that reveal insights beyond individual behavior. Insurers can identify regional risk trends, anticipate traffic congestion, forecast weather impacts, or detect fraud rings operating across borders. Public agencies can use aggregated telematics data to design safer roads and improve infrastructure planning. When managed responsibly, this shared intelligence benefits not only insurers and policyholders but entire societies.

The relationship between telematics and artificial intelligence is one of mutual enhancement. AI gives meaning to the raw data that telematics generates, while telematics provides the continuous input that AI needs to learn and adapt. Without AI, telematics would produce more data than humans could analyze. Without telematics, AI would lack the real-time information required to make accurate predictions. Together they create a cycle of intelligence where observation and action feed one another.

For example, predictive models built from telematics data can identify drivers whose behavior indicates fatigue or distraction. These models can then send automated alerts through mobile applications or dashboard notifications, preventing potential accidents. The same data can be aggregated to help city planners understand high-risk intersections or dangerous time periods. Over time, AI systems refine their predictions by learning from new events, improving precision without additional programming. This ability to evolve is what makes the combination of AI and telematics so powerful.

The value of this intelligence also extends to strategic decision-making. Insurers use predictive analytics to anticipate portfolio performance, identify high-risk regions, and develop new products. By connecting telematics insights with financial and demographic data, companies can uncover patterns that reveal market opportunities. For instance, they might find that a particular region has a high rate of safe driving but low insurance coverage, signaling an opportunity for expansion. AI-assisted telematics transforms abstract information into actionable business intelligence.

Telematics is still evolving. As vehicles, homes, and cities become smarter, the scope of connected data will expand exponentially. Future systems will integrate telematics with blockchain for secure record keeping and with quantum computing for faster analysis of complex datasets. Cross-sector collaboration between insurers, automakers, and technology companies will produce standardized ecosystems that share data transparently while maintaining privacy.

The promise of telematics lies in its ability to humanize data. It turns numbers into narratives that reflect real choices, actions, and risks. It allows insurers to see people not as statistics but as participants in a living system of cause and effect. When combined with ethical governance and advanced analytics, telematics can create a world where insurance is proactive, personalized, and fair. It is a technology that measures not only how people drive but how societies evolve.

The data-driven ecosystem of telematics represents a new chapter in global insurance. It challenges old assumptions, invites collaboration, and redefines trust in the digital age. It is not just a technological tool but a philosophy that transforms how risk is understood, managed, and shared. The true success of telematics will not be measured by the amount of data collected but by how wisely that data is used to make life safer, fairer, and more sustainable for all.

2.1 Regulation and Ethical Governance in Telematics

The rapid adoption of telematics across insurance markets has raised critical questions about privacy, fairness, and regulatory responsibility. While the technology enables transparency and precision, it also introduces an unprecedented level of surveillance into people's daily lives. The ethical challenge lies in finding a balance between innovation and individual rights. Insurers, regulators, and policymakers must work together to establish clear rules that define how data is collected, stored, and shared.

Regulation plays a decisive role in maintaining public trust. Without it, telematics could easily become intrusive or discriminatory. Customers must know that their data is used only for legitimate purposes such as risk assessment, claims accuracy, and safety enhancement. Consent must be informed, not hidden in complex policy language. Regulators in many countries have begun developing frameworks that mirror this approach. In Europe, the General Data Protection Regulation has become a global reference point. It enforces principles of data minimization, purpose limitation, and accountability. In Nigeria, the National Data Protection Regulation outlines similar obligations for organizations handling personal information.

Ethical governance must go beyond compliance. It should become a cultural value within organizations. Telematics systems must be designed to respect human dignity and fairness from the outset. This means ensuring that algorithms do not reinforce social or economic biases. If two drivers exhibit the same safe behavior, their premiums should reflect that fact regardless of location or socioeconomic background. To achieve such fairness, insurers must audit their AI models regularly and invite external oversight. Ethical boards composed of technologists, legal experts, and civil society representatives can help ensure that innovation remains aligned with societal values.

Transparency is equally important. Customers should have access to the data that influences their policies and the ability to correct errors if necessary. Insurers that allow policyholders to view and understand their data build stronger loyalty and credibility. Public awareness campaigns can further demystify telematics by showing its benefits in safety and cost reduction. When people see that technology works for them rather than against them, resistance fades. Ethical telematics therefore becomes not a constraint but a foundation for sustainable innovation.

2.2 Integration of Telematics with Global Insurance Models

Telematics is not confined to one country or market. It is rapidly becoming the foundation of a connected global insurance infrastructure. The same sensors and analytics platforms used in Lagos or Nairobi are also deployed in London, Singapore, and New York. Yet, the level of maturity and accessibility varies across regions. Integrating telematics into global insurance models requires a harmonized approach to data standards, interoperability, and risk sharing.

Global insurers face the challenge of operating across multiple jurisdictions with differing regulations, privacy expectations, and technological readiness. A system that complies with European law may not automatically meet the requirements of Asian or African regulators. To overcome these barriers, multinational insurers are developing unified frameworks for data management that adapt to local contexts while maintaining global consistency. Cloud-based architectures enable this flexibility by centralizing analytics while keeping sensitive data within national boundaries when required.

International collaboration is essential to unlocking the full value of telematics. Reinsurers, brokers, and underwriting networks can use shared telematics data to model risk across continents. For example, by comparing driver behavior patterns from multiple countries, analysts can identify cultural or environmental factors that influence accidents. Similarly, climate-sensitive telematics data can support agricultural insurers working in diverse regions. This cross-pollination of information improves the accuracy of global pricing and reinsurance strategies.

Integration also enhances innovation in product design. Multinational fleets or logistics companies can manage unified insurance policies across borders using a single telematics platform. A truck moving from Nigeria to Ghana can remain under continuous coverage, with risk assessments updating automatically as the journey progresses. This level of integration reduces administrative complexity and improves cost efficiency. It also allows insurers to provide services that reflect real operational realities instead of fragmented regional assumptions.

Cultural adaptation remains a vital factor in global implementation. While data may be universal, its interpretation is not. Driving behavior in densely populated cities differs from that in open highways. Climatic conditions, road infrastructure, and local habits all influence how telematics data should be read. Successful global models must account for these nuances. The goal is not to impose uniformity but to establish systems that learn from diversity.

The integration of telematics with global insurance models signals a future where data flows freely yet responsibly across borders. It creates a network where every piece of information contributes to a larger understanding of risk. The insurance industry is evolving into a knowledge-driven ecosystem where insights generated in one part of the world can improve safety, pricing, and service elsewhere. The ultimate success of this transformation will depend on cooperation, ethics, and the shared belief that technology, when guided by fairness, can make protection truly universal.

Chapter 3 SECURE DATA ANALYSIS IN CLOUD ENVIRONMENTS

The shift toward cloud computing has fundamentally changed how insurance organizations store, process, and analyze data. What once required large on-premise servers and manual backups can now be managed with distributed systems that operate across multiple regions. This transformation has enabled the speed and scale necessary for artificial intelligence and telematics to thrive, but it has also introduced new layers of responsibility. In an industry built on trust, the integrity and security of data determine both credibility and survival. Secure data analysis in cloud environments has therefore become one of the most critical foundations of smart insurance.

In traditional settings, insurers handled limited data streams such as policy details, claim histories, and actuarial statistics. The arrival of telematics, connected devices, and real-time analytics changed that completely. Every minute, vast amounts of information flow from vehicles, sensors, mobile applications, and partner systems into centralized platforms. This data is stored, organized, and interpreted in the cloud. While the cloud provides scalability, flexibility, and computational power, it also exposes data to risks that did not exist in isolated systems. Issues of privacy, unauthorized access, and cross-border data transfer must now be addressed with precision and foresight.

The first pillar of secure cloud analysis is architecture. A robust cloud system must be designed with defense in depth, meaning multiple layers of protection at every stage of data handling. Encryption ensures that even if information is intercepted, it remains unreadable. Access controls verify that only authorized users or applications can retrieve sensitive data. Logging and monitoring systems detect unusual activity, providing early warnings against intrusion. Modern insurers deploy these controls not as optional features but as integral parts of system design. Cloud service providers such as Amazon Web Services, Microsoft Azure, and Google Cloud offer built-in compliance tools that align with global security standards, yet the ultimate responsibility for data integrity rests with the insurer.

Data governance forms the second pillar of security. Governance defines how data is collected, classified, stored, and disposed of.

Without it, even the most advanced infrastructure can become vulnerable. Insurers must categorize their data according to sensitivity, ensuring that personally identifiable information receives the highest level of protection. Access policies must be clearly documented, with audit trails that show who accessed what data and when. Periodic risk assessments help identify weaknesses before they become breaches. Data governance also includes lifecycle management, ensuring that obsolete or redundant information is securely deleted to reduce exposure.

Another important component of secure cloud analysis is compliance. Insurance operates within some of the most regulated environments in the world. National and international frameworks such as GDPR in Europe, HIPAA in the United States, and NDPR in Nigeria set strict rules for data handling. Compliance requires more than ticking checkboxes. It demands continuous adaptation as regulations evolve and new risks emerge. Multinational insurers face additional complexity because they handle data across jurisdictions with different laws. Cloud systems must therefore include data localization capabilities, allowing information to remain within national borders when required by law. Non-compliance can result in legal penalties and loss of customer confidence, making regulatory alignment both a legal and business necessity.

In addition to these structural safeguards, secure data analysis depends on strong operational discipline. Human error remains one of the leading causes of data breaches. A misplaced credential, an unsecured endpoint, or a weak password can compromise entire systems. Organizations must cultivate a culture of security awareness across all departments. Employees should be trained regularly on cybersecurity practices such as identifying phishing attempts, managing credentials, and using encryption tools properly. When everyone understands that data security is a shared responsibility, the overall resilience of the organization improves dramatically.

Beyond protecting data, insurers must also ensure the accuracy and reliability of the analysis derived from it. Integrity verification is crucial because tampered or corrupted data can mislead predictive models, resulting in flawed pricing or risk assessments. Techniques such as checksum validation, blockchain-based data lineage, and secure APIs help maintain authenticity across distributed networks. Real-time validation processes confirm that incoming telematics data has not been altered during transmission. Insurers who fail to guarantee data authenticity risk financial losses and regulatory scrutiny.

Cloud environments have also redefined the meaning of collaboration. In the past, insurers, brokers, and reinsurers operated in largely separate technological silos. Today, they often share data streams and analytical tools through secure cloud-based ecosystems. This interconnectivity allows faster coordination during claim settlements, fraud detection, and catastrophe modeling. However, it also increases the number of access points that must be protected. Shared environments must use segmentation techniques that isolate sensitive information and apply encryption during both transfer and storage. Mutual trust agreements and security certifications become essential in maintaining accountability across organizational boundaries.

An often overlooked dimension of secure cloud analysis is resilience. Insurance companies must not only protect against cyberattacks but also prepare for system failures and natural disasters. Cloud infrastructure offers redundancy through multiple data centers in different locations. If one center is compromised, operations can continue from another without loss of service. Regular disaster recovery tests and business continuity plans ensure that critical operations can withstand disruptions. The ability to recover quickly is as important as the ability to prevent breaches.

The integration of artificial intelligence within cloud environments further complicates the security landscape. AI models require vast datasets for training and testing, some of which may contain sensitive personal information. If this data is not properly anonymized, it can expose individuals to privacy risks. Ethical AI design therefore includes security as a fundamental principle. Models must be trained with data that is representative but protected. Techniques such as differential privacy and federated learning are emerging as solutions that allow AI to learn from distributed data without centralizing it. This approach minimizes exposure while maintaining analytical power.

While technology provides the tools, true data security is ultimately a question of trust. Customers share their information with insurers because they believe it will be used responsibly. Every breach undermines that belief. Trust cannot be rebuilt through technology alone; it requires consistent transparency. Insurers should communicate their data protection measures clearly, explaining how information is used and what steps are taken to prevent misuse. When clients understand that their data is treated with respect and care, loyalty strengthens and brand reputation grows.

The benefits of secure cloud analysis extend beyond protection. Security also enables innovation. A strong foundation of trust allows insurers to experiment with new analytics models, integrate third-party data sources, and develop personalized products without fear of compromising privacy. For example, predictive analytics can be expanded to include external data such as weather reports, economic indicators, or social sentiment analysis. When such integration occurs within a secure framework, the resulting insights are both powerful and compliant. Security and innovation, often perceived as opposites, are in fact interdependent.

In developing markets, cloud-based security frameworks are accelerating modernization. Many local insurers lack the resources to build advanced in-house infrastructure. Cloud solutions allow them to adopt global best practices without massive upfront investment. Providers offer scalable platforms that meet international standards for encryption, backup, and compliance. This democratization of technology enables smaller firms to compete effectively while maintaining the same level of protection as larger organizations. It also strengthens the overall financial ecosystem by raising industry-wide security expectations.

As the volume of data continues to expand, the importance of secure analysis will only increase. The future of smart insurance depends not just on how much data is collected but on how responsibly it is managed. The cloud offers infinite potential, but that potential can only be realized when built on a foundation of security, governance, and ethical stewardship. Insurance organizations that understand this will not only survive but lead in the next era of digital risk management. They will earn trust not through slogans but through consistent, verifiable protection of the most valuable asset in the modern world: data.

3.1 Data Sovereignty and Cross-Border Compliance

One of the most complex issues in secure cloud analysis is the question of data sovereignty. As insurers expand across borders, the data they collect often travels through multiple jurisdictions, each with its own laws governing storage, access, and transfer. Data sovereignty refers to the concept that information is subject to the laws of the country where it is located. This becomes critical in insurance, where customer data may reside in one country while the analytics systems processing it operate in another.

Cloud computing challenges traditional interpretations of jurisdiction. A policyholder in Lagos may have their data hosted on servers in Frankfurt or Singapore. Each of these locations imposes different legal obligations on the insurer regarding retention, privacy, and third-party access. Regulators are increasingly aware of this complexity and are requiring organizations to maintain transparency about where their data resides. Some countries mandate that sensitive or financial information be stored locally to prevent unauthorized foreign access. Others allow cross-border transfer only when adequate safeguards are in place.

For global insurers, compliance involves designing hybrid cloud systems that balance flexibility with legal certainty. Data localization tools allow sensitive information to remain within national borders, while anonymized datasets can be transmitted securely for analysis abroad. The challenge is maintaining analytical continuity without breaching any jurisdictional boundaries. This requires detailed documentation of data flows, third-party contracts that include security clauses, and regular audits to ensure adherence.

Cross-border compliance is not only a legal matter but also a matter of trust. Customers must be confident that their information is protected regardless of where it travels. Public disclosure of data handling practices strengthens this trust. When policyholders understand that their data is treated with equal care in every location, confidence in digital insurance systems grows. In this sense, respecting sovereignty does not restrict innovation; it reinforces legitimacy. The companies that master this balance will define the next phase of global smart insurance.

3.2 The Human Factor in Cloud Security Governance

Technology may create the framework for cloud security, but people determine its success. Even the most advanced encryption systems cannot compensate for negligence, poor training, or lack of accountability. Human error remains the single largest cause of security breaches worldwide. In the context of insurance, where data represents financial credibility, a single mistake can trigger massive financial and reputational damage. The human factor in governance therefore deserves as much attention as the technical aspects of protection.

Cloud environments require a security culture that extends beyond the IT department. Every employee who handles data, from call center staff to senior executives, must understand their role in maintaining confidentiality. Awareness programs, simulations, and regular training sessions help build instinctive security behavior. Staff must learn to identify phishing emails, manage passwords securely, and avoid exposing information through social engineering attacks. An organization's weakest point is often not its software but its untrained personnel.

Leadership also plays a critical role. Executives must treat cybersecurity as a strategic priority rather than an operational afterthought. Decisions about partnerships, product launches, and digital investments should include risk assessments at the planning stage. This proactive mindset turns security from a defensive measure into a competitive advantage. Customers trust companies that demonstrate visible commitment to safeguarding information.

Insurers can further strengthen governance by establishing clear accountability structures. Each department should have designated security champions who coordinate compliance activities and report incidents promptly. The creation of a Chief Information Security Officer or equivalent role ensures that cybersecurity receives executive-level oversight. Reporting lines should be transparent, and communication between technical teams and management must be frequent and clear.

Another important dimension of human governance is collaboration. Cloud security cannot operate in isolation. It requires cooperation among insurers, regulators, service providers, and policyholders. Information sharing about emerging threats and best practices helps the entire ecosystem become more resilient. Forums, industry associations, and academic partnerships play a vital role in this collective defense.

At the heart of this human-centered approach lies accountability. Every person with access to data must feel responsible for its protection. Security cannot be outsourced entirely to machines or vendors. It is a discipline of vigilance, decision-making, and ethical judgment. When employees internalize these values, organizations gain not only stronger defenses but also a culture of integrity.

Ultimately, the human factor transforms cloud security from a technical function into a moral one. Data represents real people with real vulnerabilities. Protecting it is not just a business obligation but a social responsibility. Insurers who embrace this mindset will stand out in an industry where trust defines every transaction. The combination of secure infrastructure and ethical human leadership will shape the future of digital insurance governance.

Chapter 4 ARTIFICIAL INTELLIGENCE AND MACHINE LEARNING IN RISK MODELING

Artificial intelligence has become the central nervous system of modern insurance. What once relied on human intuition and mathematical probability has evolved into a world of predictive algorithms that learn, adapt, and refine themselves over time. Insurance companies are no longer simply reacting to risk; they are forecasting it with unprecedented accuracy. Through artificial intelligence and machine learning, insurers can analyze massive datasets drawn from telematics, financial records, customer interactions, and environmental indicators. This intelligence allows them to understand not only what has happened but what is most likely to happen next.

Machine learning, the subset of artificial intelligence responsible for self-improving algorithms, thrives on data. The more quality data it receives, the more precise its predictions become. In insurance, this means that every claim, every policy, and every behavioral record contributes to a model that becomes smarter with time. These models identify correlations invisible to human analysts. For example, a machine learning system may discover that certain combinations of road type, weather condition, and time of day increase the likelihood of an accident more than any single factor alone. Such findings can shape pricing strategies, safety recommendations, and underwriting decisions.

The rise of AI in insurance has introduced predictive modeling as a core function rather than a supporting tool. Predictive models simulate various future outcomes using historical and real-time data. They calculate the probability of claims, defaults, or fraudulent activity. In health insurance, they can even forecast the likelihood of medical events based on lifestyle data from wearable devices. These predictions are not absolute but probabilistic, giving insurers the ability to make data-driven judgments rather than rely on assumptions. As predictive systems evolve, the boundary between risk assessment and risk prevention continues to blur.

The sophistication of modern models lies in their ability to combine different types of data. Structured data such as policy records and financial statements merge with unstructured data such as social media posts, voice recordings, and satellite images.

Natural language processing enables computers to read and interpret claim descriptions or customer feedback, identifying potential anomalies or emerging trends. Computer vision allows algorithms to evaluate photographs of vehicle damage or property loss, providing instant claim estimates that once took hours or days. Through these methods, AI not only speeds up operations but transforms the very texture of decision-making in insurance.

Fraud detection is one of the areas where machine learning has proven most effective. Traditional fraud prevention relied heavily on manual audits and pattern recognition based on static rules. Fraudsters quickly learned how to bypass these systems. AI changed the equation by introducing adaptive models that learn continuously from new behavior. Each transaction, claim, or payment is analyzed in real time, and any deviation from expected patterns triggers an alert. Neural networks can distinguish between normal variations and suspicious anomalies, reducing false positives and allowing investigators to focus on genuine threats. This ability to learn from evolving tactics has made AI one of the strongest defenses against financial crime in the insurance sector.

Underwriting has also been transformed. Previously, underwriters used historical averages to determine pricing, often leading to generalized risk categories that treated very different customers the same way. Machine learning introduces dynamic pricing models that evaluate individuals or businesses based on specific data attributes. A driver who consistently follows speed limits or avoids high-risk routes receives a lower premium. Similarly, a manufacturing firm that maintains strong safety records and monitors equipment performance may enjoy reduced rates. The result is fairness, efficiency, and stronger alignment between price and behavior. This approach not only benefits insurers but also encourages clients to engage in safer, more responsible practices.

Despite its power, AI in risk modeling must be approached with caution. Algorithms are only as unbiased as the data they are trained on. Historical datasets may contain hidden prejudices that reflect social or economic disparities. If left unchecked, these biases can lead to unfair outcomes. For instance, if historical data overrepresents claims from certain neighborhoods due to unequal policing or infrastructure, the AI may assign higher premiums to residents there regardless of individual behavior. Ethical data governance therefore becomes a cornerstone of AI deployment. Insurers must ensure that their models are transparent, explainable, and subject to periodic review by human experts. Explainable AI techniques allow analysts to understand how decisions are made, reducing the risk of invisible discrimination.

The transition from manual analysis to machine learning also changes the role of human professionals. Underwriters, actuaries, and analysts are not being replaced but empowered. Their expertise now focuses on model validation, ethical oversight, and strategic interpretation rather than repetitive computation. Humans provide the moral and contextual understanding that machines lack. For example, a predictive model may flag a particular case as high-risk, but a human underwriter may recognize contextual details that the algorithm cannot interpret. The future of risk modeling depends on this partnership between machine precision and human judgment.

From an operational perspective, AI-driven models require significant computing power and robust infrastructure. Cloud platforms have become indispensable for training and deploying models at scale. Distributed computing allows organizations to process terabytes of data efficiently, while containerization tools ensure that models remain portable across environments. Continuous monitoring is also vital. Models must be retrained regularly as new data becomes available. Failure to update algorithms can result in drift, where predictions gradually lose accuracy over time. Maintaining this cycle of retraining and validation ensures that risk assessments remain current and reliable.

Artificial intelligence has also improved catastrophe modeling, an area critical to reinsurance and global risk management. By integrating satellite imagery, weather forecasts, and historical disaster data, AI can simulate potential outcomes for hurricanes, floods, or wildfires. These simulations help insurers anticipate losses and allocate capital more effectively. Machine learning also assists in post-event analysis, allowing insurers to refine their models based on real outcomes. The goal is not only to react faster but to predict better, building systems resilient enough to withstand uncertainty.

The integration of AI with telematics data represents one of the most powerful developments in predictive risk assessment. Telematics provides a continuous stream of behavioral data, while AI converts that data into real-time insights. Together, they form a dynamic feedback system that supports proactive decision-making. For example, AI can detect risky driving habits early and send personalized feedback through mobile apps. It can identify fleets showing patterns of fatigue or maintenance neglect, allowing interventions before accidents occur. This collaboration between machine intelligence and behavioral data turns risk management into an ongoing, interactive process rather than a static calculation.

AI has also begun to influence customer experience in ways that extend beyond pricing and claims. Chatbots and virtual assistants powered by natural language understanding provide 24-hour support, answering questions, processing simple claims, or recommending coverage adjustments. Recommendation engines analyze user behavior to suggest policies suited to individual needs. These systems make insurance more accessible and responsive, especially to younger generations accustomed to digital convenience. However, automation must never come at the expense of empathy. The best AI systems complement, not replace, human communication by ensuring that customers feel heard, understood, and valued.

Ethical AI also demands transparency. Policyholders deserve to know when they are interacting with automated systems and how their data contributes to decisions. Openness builds trust and reduces suspicion of algorithmic manipulation. Some insurers have begun publishing model transparency reports that describe the types of data used, the purpose of analysis, and the safeguards in place to prevent misuse. Such initiatives signal a shift toward accountability in digital decision-making. In the long term, transparent AI practices will become a regulatory expectation rather than a voluntary gesture.

The economic impact of AI on insurance is already evident. Companies that have adopted data-driven risk models report improved accuracy in pricing, faster claim resolutions, and reduced fraud costs. The efficiencies gained translate into competitive advantage and greater customer satisfaction. Yet the long-term sustainability of AI depends on continuous evaluation of its social effects. Technology must enhance fairness and inclusion rather than deepen inequality. By making risk more measurable, AI can also make protection more universal, extending insurance access to underserved populations who were previously excluded due to lack of data.

Artificial intelligence and machine learning have therefore redefined the boundaries of possibility in risk modeling. They have replaced assumption with analysis, intuition with insight, and reaction with prediction. However, the essence of insurance remains the same: protection. Technology must serve that mission by making coverage more accurate, equitable, and secure. When properly governed, AI does not diminish the human role in insurance; it amplifies it. It transforms data into understanding and understanding into confidence. The ultimate purpose of artificial intelligence in risk modeling is not only to predict loss but to empower people and institutions to live, work, and build with greater certainty in an uncertain world.

4.1 Adaptive Learning Systems and Model Evolution

Artificial intelligence in insurance does not remain static. Unlike traditional actuarial models that are built once and applied repeatedly, AI-driven systems evolve continuously. Adaptive learning allows algorithms to improve through constant exposure to new information. Every policy renewal, claim settlement, or behavioral update enriches the dataset that feeds predictive models. This flow of real-world information ensures that risk assessments remain relevant in changing conditions.

For instance, driving behaviors may shift over time due to new traffic regulations, economic factors, or urban development. A static model would struggle to accommodate such transitions, but an adaptive system recalibrates automatically. It identifies new correlations, removes outdated assumptions, and learns from exceptions that do not fit established patterns. This adaptability turns AI from a reactive system into a self-optimizing one.

Adaptive learning also helps mitigate model fatigue. When data patterns change significantly, models may begin to lose accuracy, a phenomenon known as drift. Continuous retraining prevents this decline. The process requires careful management to ensure that the system learns correctly without inheriting noise or bias from recent anomalies. Governance teams typically establish thresholds that trigger retraining only when statistically significant shifts occur. In this way, insurers maintain both consistency and innovation in their predictive processes.

Another dimension of adaptation involves reinforcement learning, where algorithms improve by simulating real-world scenarios and adjusting decisions based on outcomes. This technique is useful in claims management and customer engagement. For example, AI models can test different approaches to claim prioritization or customer outreach, learning over time which strategies produce the best satisfaction and retention rates. The future of insurance modeling will depend on such self-learning systems that refine themselves without manual reprogramming.

4.2 AI Ethics and Accountability in Decision Automation

The integration of artificial intelligence into financial decision-making carries immense ethical responsibility. Insurance deals directly with people's livelihoods, property, and well-being. Every automated decision has a real human impact, and this makes accountability crucial. As predictive models take on more authority in underwriting and claims approval, the need for ethical oversight becomes non-negotiable.

Ethical AI begins with transparency. Customers have the right to know when an algorithm influences their premium, claim approval, or risk score. Opacity erodes trust, while openness strengthens it. Insurers must be able to explain in plain language why a particular decision was made. Explainable AI techniques make this possible by revealing which variables contributed most to a prediction. This ensures that outcomes are not only accurate but also understandable.

Fairness is another cornerstone of AI ethics. Bias can enter a model through skewed data, incomplete sampling, or improper feature selection. A biased dataset can perpetuate systemic inequalities. Insurers must conduct fairness audits that test how their models perform across different demographic groups. If discrepancies are found, adjustments must be made either to the data or to the algorithm's weighting system. Ethical governance requires a combination of technical correction and moral awareness.

Accountability extends to governance structures. Many leading insurers now maintain AI ethics committees responsible for reviewing algorithms before deployment. These committees include data scientists, actuaries, legal experts, and external advisors. Their role is to ensure that each model aligns with company values, regulatory expectations, and social norms.

Ethical frameworks such as the OECD AI Principles and ISO standards for AI risk management are increasingly guiding these reviews.

Finally, insurers must plan for responsibility in failure. No model is infallible. When an algorithm produces an incorrect or harmful decision, there must be a clear mechanism for redress. Human oversight ensures that errors are corrected and lessons are learned. In the long term, ethical AI will not be defined by perfection but by accountability and the willingness to improve.

4.3 AI-Powered Scenario Simulation and Strategic Forecasting

Risk is not limited to what can be observed; it often lies in what could happen. Artificial intelligence allows insurers to explore this uncertainty through scenario simulation and strategic forecasting. Using advanced computational models, insurers can simulate thousands of possible futures to evaluate how different factors might influence outcomes. These simulations combine historical data with hypothetical variables such as economic shifts, climate change, or market disruption.

In reinsurance, scenario modeling helps assess large-scale catastrophes. AI systems can generate synthetic hurricane or flood events based on meteorological data and climate projections. They estimate potential damages, simulate claims distribution, and test capital adequacy under extreme conditions.

This allows insurers to prepare financially for disasters that have not yet occurred. Machine learning refines these simulations over time, learning from each real event to produce more accurate future forecasts.

Financial forecasting also benefits from AI-driven simulation. Predictive models can estimate the impact of inflation, currency fluctuations, or interest rate changes on claim reserves and investment portfolios. Strategic planners use these insights to optimize asset allocation and premium structures. The combination of risk modeling and financial forecasting enables insurance companies to remain stable even in volatile markets.

Scenario simulation also supports policy innovation. Insurers can test the viability of new products virtually before launching them. For instance, an AI model may simulate how a new type of digital health insurance would perform across age groups or geographic regions. It can identify risk clusters, pricing inefficiencies, or potential compliance issues before the product enters the market. This approach reduces trial-and-error costs and accelerates innovation cycles.

In a broader sense, AI-powered simulation strengthens resilience. It allows organizations to anticipate not only economic or environmental shocks but also social and technological trends. As automation spreads and customer expectations evolve, scenario forecasting helps insurers remain adaptable. The predictive insight gained from simulation becomes a strategic compass, guiding decisions that safeguard profitability while maintaining fairness and trust.

Chapter 5 FINANCIAL DATA ANALYTICS AND PROFITABILITY DASHBOARDS

Financial data analytics has become the compass guiding the modern insurance enterprise. In a world where decisions must be made quickly and precisely, insurers can no longer depend on intuition or static reports. They need live intelligence, numbers that tell a story, metrics that reveal behavior, and models that predict the future. Financial analytics serves as the backbone of this intelligence. It connects operational performance with strategic foresight, allowing organizations to see not just where they stand but where they are headed.

Insurance is a business of balance. It relies on maintaining equilibrium between premium income and claim obligations, between risk exposure and capital reserves. In the past, this balance was tracked through spreadsheets, quarterly reports, and manual reconciliation. Those methods are now obsolete. The integration of artificial intelligence, big data, and automation has turned financial analytics into a continuous process. Every policy, payment, and claim generates new information that feeds into real-time dashboards. Executives, actuaries, and analysts can observe company performance as it happens, rather than after it has already shifted.

Profitability dashboards are at the heart of this transformation. They translate complex financial data into visual insights that support decision-making. A well-designed dashboard integrates multiple layers of information; premium growth, loss ratios, expense trends, and investment performance into a single, comprehensible interface. By interacting with these tools, managers can drill down from macro-level performance to micro-level transactions. They can identify which products, regions, or customer segments are driving profit and which are draining resources. This visibility empowers leadership to respond swiftly to emerging opportunities and threats.

The architecture of a financial analytics system relies on integration. Data flows from various sources: underwriting systems, claims databases, customer relationship platforms, and external market feeds. These are consolidated in a data warehouse or cloud-based environment where analytics engines can access them. Predictive algorithms then process the information to detect anomalies, forecast future performance, and recommend corrective actions. The result is a system that moves beyond reporting into intelligent guidance.

At the operational level, analytics supports performance tracking. Key performance indicators such as combined ratio, return on equity, claim frequency, and expense ratio are monitored continuously. Machine learning models detect patterns that might indicate emerging risks, such as an increase in fraudulent claims or declining retention in specific customer segments. By catching these trends early, insurers can adjust pricing, marketing, or product design before financial impact grows severe.

Financial analytics also strengthens underwriting discipline. By linking risk assessment data with profitability metrics, insurers can determine which policy types contribute most to long-term success. For instance, a particular class of motor insurance might appear profitable at first glance but could carry high claim volatility. Advanced analytics highlights these inconsistencies, allowing underwriters to refine criteria or adjust coverage terms. This integration ensures that underwriting decisions align with corporate financial goals rather than short-term targets.

Claims management represents another area of transformation. Claims are the largest cost center in any insurance business, and efficient management directly influences profitability. Predictive analytics helps estimate claim costs more accurately, allocate reserves appropriately, and detect potential overpayments. Dashboards can display claims by type, region, and settlement time, giving managers a clear picture of operational efficiency. Combined with automation tools, this reduces processing time, improves customer satisfaction, and protects margins.

Investment performance is equally important. Insurers operate as both risk managers and financial investors, allocating premiums into diverse portfolios to generate returns. Financial analytics provides insight into portfolio composition, market exposure, and capital adequacy. Real-time monitoring of asset performance enables proactive rebalancing in response to market fluctuations. Predictive forecasting tools assess how economic indicators such as inflation or interest rate changes may affect investment income. This forward-looking approach allows insurers to maintain solvency while optimizing returns.

Data visualization is what makes financial analytics truly actionable. Numbers alone can overwhelm even experienced professionals. Visualization tools such as heat maps, trend lines, and comparative graphs convert complexity into clarity. For example, a dashboard might use color-coded indicators to show profitability by region or line of business. A sudden shift in color signals where attention is needed. Interactive filters allow users to isolate data by time, geography, or customer segment, turning static information into strategic insight.

Beyond profitability, financial analytics improves transparency and accountability. Regulators require insurers to demonstrate sound financial management and compliance with solvency standards. Automated dashboards provide the necessary audit trails, ensuring that every figure is traceable to its source. This not only supports compliance but builds confidence among investors, partners, and policyholders. Trust in an insurer's financial integrity is essential for market stability, and data-driven transparency reinforces that trust.

The democratization of analytics has also changed how teams collaborate. Previously, financial data was controlled by small departments of analysts and actuaries. Today, self-service dashboards allow managers, marketers, and underwriters to explore data directly. This decentralization encourages innovation and faster decision-making. However, it also demands governance. Access levels must be defined to prevent misuse or misinterpretation of data. When balance is achieved, organizations benefit from collective intelligence—an environment where insights flow freely while security remains intact.

Financial data analytics is also deeply connected to customer experience. By examining profitability by customer segment, insurers can identify patterns that reveal loyalty, satisfaction, or churn. Predictive models forecast which clients are likely to renew and which may leave. Targeted retention campaigns based on these insights save resources and maintain revenue stability. Personalization extends beyond marketing; it influences product design and pricing strategies that reflect real value rather than generalized averages.

The cultural shift toward data-driven decision-making cannot be overstated. Companies that integrate analytics into their daily operations move from reactive management to proactive leadership. Decisions are supported by evidence rather than speculation, and performance becomes measurable at every level. The mindset changes from "What happened?" to "What is happening?" and ultimately to "What should we do next?" This evolution positions analytics not as a department but as the foundation of organizational intelligence.

Financial analytics and profitability dashboards are not static achievements; they are evolving ecosystems. As artificial intelligence continues to mature, these systems will gain cognitive capabilities—learning from results, adapting to market conditions, and offering prescriptive recommendations.

Dashboards will no longer just display information but will advise on actions. They will become digital advisors capable of guiding strategy in real time.

Ultimately, the goal of financial data analytics in insurance is not simply to increase profit but to ensure sustainability. A profitable company without insight can fail suddenly, while an informed company can endure volatility with resilience. Data gives insurers the power to see risk before it becomes loss and opportunity before it becomes competition. Financial analytics turns information into foresight and foresight into stability.

The most successful insurers of the future will be those that treat data as a living asset, dashboards as instruments of truth, and analytics as the language of leadership. When used responsibly, financial intelligence becomes not just a tool for counting profits but a compass for navigating uncertainty. It brings clarity where there is complexity and transforms information into wisdom, an essential quality for thriving in a financial world defined by speed, precision, and continuous change.

5.1 Performance Measurement Techniques in Modern Insurance

Performance measurement is the heartbeat of financial analytics. It allows insurers to understand whether their strategies are working, whether risk is being priced correctly, and whether operational costs are justified by outcomes. In earlier decades, performance evaluation depended on static metrics such as combined ratio or net underwriting income. These indicators remain relevant, but the speed and complexity of modern markets have demanded more dynamic tools.

Advanced performance measurement combines financial data with operational intelligence. Machine learning models now assist in calculating predictive versions of key performance indicators. Instead of showing what a company achieved last quarter, these models forecast what will likely happen next. For example, a predictive combined ratio might estimate future claims expenses based on current driving behavior data from telematics. Similarly, expected return on equity can be simulated under different economic conditions to anticipate capital needs.

Another evolution is the shift from isolated metrics to composite indexes. Insurers now evaluate profitability through multidimensional lenses that consider financial, behavioral, and strategic data simultaneously. A composite performance index may combine metrics such as loss ratio, policy renewal rate, customer satisfaction, and digital adoption rate. The resulting score gives executives a more holistic view of organizational health.

Granularity is also transforming how performance is tracked. Dashboards can now segment data by agent, region, product line, or customer type. Managers can see which areas outperform and which require intervention. This transparency eliminates guesswork. Every department becomes accountable for results backed by real evidence. As artificial intelligence becomes more embedded in financial systems, these measurement techniques will grow even more refined, turning performance tracking into an intelligent conversation between data and decision-makers.

5.2 Predictive Profitability Modeling and Forecasting

Profitability in insurance has always been difficult to predict. Market volatility, claims unpredictability, and regulatory changes make forecasting challenging. Artificial intelligence and advanced analytics have begun to solve this problem through predictive profitability modeling. These models combine historical data with forward-looking variables to simulate different financial outcomes. The goal is not only to measure profit but to understand the forces that shape it.

Predictive profitability models analyze the interactions between premiums, claims, investments, and operational costs. For instance, they can estimate how a five percent increase in motor claims frequency will affect net margins or how rising interest rates might influence investment income. These simulations help insurers make informed strategic adjustments. They can increase reserves, adjust pricing, or modify product portfolios before challenges escalate.

One of the most powerful tools in this domain is sensitivity analysis. This technique tests how sensitive profitability is to individual variables. It reveals which factors exert the strongest influence on outcomes and where management should focus its attention. When combined with Monte Carlo simulation, it produces a range of possible futures rather than a single forecast. This approach aligns perfectly with the probabilistic nature of insurance, where uncertainty is inherent.

Scenario-based forecasting also enhances strategic resilience. Using predictive models, companies can simulate crises such as cyberattacks, natural disasters, or sudden market downturns. By understanding potential losses and recovery times, they can design contingency plans that protect both capital and reputation. The same predictive frameworks can be used positively to identify opportunities, such as entering new markets or launching innovative products. Predictive profitability modeling turns uncertainty from a threat into an asset by quantifying it.

These systems also improve communication between departments. Finance teams, underwriters, and claims managers can all visualize how their actions affect the company's profitability in real time. Predictive forecasting breaks organizational silos by linking cause and effect across the entire insurance value chain. Decisions that were once based on intuition are now guided by scientific precision.

5.3 Visualization Standards and Financial Storytelling

The explosion of data in insurance would mean little without effective communication. Visualization is what converts raw numbers into understanding. A well-crafted dashboard not only informs but persuades. It tells a story about where the company stands and where it is going. The art of financial storytelling through visualization has become a strategic skill as important as the analysis itself.

Effective visualization in insurance follows three guiding principles: clarity, consistency, and context. Clarity ensures that complex information is presented in an intuitive format. Consistency ensures that metrics are comparable across time and departments. Context ensures that numbers are interpreted correctly rather than in isolation. Dashboards that follow these principles allow decision-makers to see both the big picture and the underlying details at a glance.

Visualization standards also involve design discipline. Every chart, color, and label must have meant. Financial dashboards typically use standardized color schemes to represent performance states green for profit growth, yellow for caution, and red for loss or risk escalation. Fonts and layouts should remain uniform across departments to maintain coherence and reduce cognitive load.

Beyond aesthetics, visualization is about storytelling. Each dashboard must answer a question or highlight a trend that leads to action. For instance, a profitability dashboard might reveal how claim frequency rises in certain regions during specific months. The visual should guide the viewer naturally from observation to insight and finally to strategy. When supported by predictive analytics, visualization becomes interactive, allowing executives to explore scenarios by adjusting variables directly on screen.

Transparency is another key element of visualization standards. Users must be able to trace each figure back to its data source. This traceability reinforces credibility and supports compliance audits. In global organizations, visualization platforms often integrate multilingual and multi-currency features to ensure inclusivity across regions.

Financial storytelling is more than presentation; it is persuasion through evidence. When leaders can visualize the company's trajectory clearly, they make decisions with confidence. Well-designed dashboards unite analytics, communication, and leadership in one frame. They turn abstract data into actionable intelligence and transform financial management into a shared narrative understood by all.

Chapter 6 PREDICTIVE TELEMATICS AND DRIVER RISK SCORING

Predictive telematics represents the point where data science meets behavioral insight. In insurance, it has shifted the perception of risk from something historical to something dynamic and continuously measurable. By merging artificial intelligence with real-time telematics data, insurers can forecast driver behavior, identify risk patterns before incidents occur, and create pricing systems rooted in fairness rather than generalization. Driver risk scoring, the practical outcome of this convergence, has become a cornerstone of modern motor insurance and fleet management worldwide.

At its core, predictive telematics uses sensor data collected from vehicles; speed, acceleration, braking intensity, cornering angles, and location, to build behavioral profiles. Each action contributes to an overall risk score that reflects how likely a driver is to be involved in an accident. Over time, as the algorithm learns from millions of driving sessions, the models become remarkably accurate. A sudden spike in harsh braking, for instance, might indicate distracted driving, while consistent speeding in high-risk zones may trigger early alerts for intervention.

Unlike conventional underwriting that relies on demographic categories such as age or gender, predictive telematics assesses individuals based on their actual habits. This approach not only reduces discrimination but encourages responsibility. Drivers who demonstrate safe and consistent behavior benefit from lower premiums, while high-risk drivers are guided toward corrective measures. The system is both preventative and educational, making insurance a partner in safety rather than a distant assessor of loss.

Telematics devices come in many forms. Early models were physical black boxes installed in vehicles, but technological progress has expanded the options. Today, mobile applications, Bluetooth sensors, and connected car systems perform the same functions with greater accuracy and convenience. These tools capture high-frequency data transmitted securely to cloud platforms, where machine learning models analyze it in real time. The outcome is a living ecosystem of risk intelligence that benefits drivers, insurers, and regulators alike.

Predictive modeling transforms telematics data into actionable insight. By combining behavioral indicators with contextual variables such as weather, traffic density, and road type, algorithms can forecast accident probability for every trip. Insurers use this predictive capability not just for pricing but for loss prevention. Fleet managers can monitor risk exposure across their drivers and vehicles, issuing proactive warnings or scheduling targeted training programs. The result is fewer accidents, lower claim costs, and improved safety standards across the board.

Driver risk scoring also strengthens claim verification. In the aftermath of an accident, telematics data provides an objective record of events. The exact time, speed, and impact angle are captured instantly, reducing disputes and expediting claims. Fraudulent claims, a persistent issue in the industry, become easier to detect when behavioral patterns contradict reported incidents. This transparency enhances trust between insurers and clients.

Telematics data also supports broader societal goals. Governments and transportation authority's use aggregated, anonymized data to identify high-risk roads, optimize traffic flow, and develop targeted safety policies. In this way, predictive telematics becomes a public good as well as a private innovation.

It enables data-driven governance while maintaining individual privacy.

The technology continues to evolve. As vehicles become more autonomous, predictive telematics will integrate with advanced driver assistance systems to create even deeper insights. Cameras, lidar sensors, and vehicle-to-infrastructure communication will produce multidimensional data that enriches risk scoring models. The ability to combine human and machine driving data will open new frontiers for understanding how different systems interact under various conditions.

Privacy and consent remain critical issues in predictive telematics. While the benefits are clear, the potential for misuse cannot be ignored. Insurers must ensure that customers understand what data is being collected and how it influences pricing. Data should be anonymized whenever possible, and storage systems must meet strict security standards. Transparent governance and communication will determine the public's long-term trust in this technology.

Driver risk scoring represents more than a technical innovation; it reflects a philosophical shift in how society defines accountability. Instead of viewing accidents as random events, insurers now understand them as measurable outcomes of behavior and environment. Predictive telematics turns driving from a static activity into a feedback-driven discipline. The road becomes a source of learning, and data becomes the teacher.

As this technology matures, it will redefine the relationship between drivers and insurers. Risk scoring will move from punitive assessment to collaborative improvement. Drivers will receive personalized coaching based on real data, fleets will gain tools for continuous optimization, and insurers will build stronger, more transparent relationships with their clients. Predictive telematics is not just about monitoring; it is about empowerment. It turns risk into knowledge, knowledge into safety, and safety into shared value.

6.1 Behavioral Insights and Algorithmic Calibration

Predictive telematics is most effective when it captures the full context of driver behavior rather than isolated data points. The science behind driver risk scoring depends on the accuracy of behavioral interpretation. Every recorded movement, an acceleration, a sharp turn, a sudden brake must be calibrated against environmental and situational variables to ensure fairness. A hard brake caused by avoiding a stray animal, for instance, should not be weighted the same as reckless speeding in traffic. Algorithmic calibration corrects these distinctions by teaching the system how to differentiate intent from circumstance.

Machine learning plays a central role in this process. Models are trained on massive datasets that include both telematics information and labeled outcomes, such as accident frequency or claim severity. As the system learns, it fine-tunes the weight assigned to different behaviors. Over time, these calibrations produce more accurate and equitable risk scores. Algorithms that once treated all high-speed driving as dangerous now distinguish between safe highway cruising and erratic urban driving. This sophistication improves customer satisfaction and ensures that premiums reflect genuine risk rather than general assumptions.

Behavioral insights derived from calibrated algorithms go beyond risk prediction. They help insurers design educational programs that encourage safer habits. Personalized driver feedback, delivered through mobile apps or in-car notifications can inform users about their risk patterns and offer tips for improvement. The approach mirrors preventive healthcare: it is better to guide than to penalize. Insurers who use behavioral analytics to empower clients foster loyalty and long-term trust.

Calibration also strengthens cross-regional fairness. Driving styles and road conditions differ widely from Lagos to London or Nairobi to New York. Algorithms must account for cultural, climatic, and infrastructural differences to avoid bias. This requires constant retraining using localized data. The success of predictive telematics depends not only on technological precision but on sensitivity to the social and environmental realities of driving across the world.

6.2 Ethics and Privacy in Driver Data Governance

The ethical dimension of predictive telematics is as important as its technical design. Every piece of telematics data; speed, location, time, and route, represents an aspect of human behavior. Collecting and processing such information carries moral responsibility. Insurers must strike a delicate balance between using data for legitimate safety and pricing improvements and respecting the privacy of individual drivers.

Ethical data governance begins with consent. Drivers should clearly understand what data is being collected, how long it will be stored, and who can access it. Consent should be active, not hidden in fine print. Transparency transforms surveillance into service by giving users confidence that their information is handled fairly. In advanced systems, customers can review their driving data, request corrections, or opt out of specific analyses. Such openness promotes trust and aligns with global privacy standards.

Data minimization is another ethical principle. Not all collected information is necessary for risk scoring. Insurers should store only what is relevant to their analytical goals and anonymize them wherever possible. This reduces exposure in case of breaches and ensures that sensitive details such as location trails cannot be traced back to individuals. Ethical governance also includes robust data security measures. Encryption, regular audits, and access restrictions are not just technical obligations but moral imperatives when human behavior is being recorded.

The use of telematics data must also avoid discrimination. Algorithms trained on biased datasets may unintentionally disadvantage certain groups or regions. Continuous fairness testing ensures that predictive models remain impartial. When ethical review teams regularly evaluate how data influences pricing and decision-making, the industry maintains accountability and public confidence.

In the long run, ethics and privacy will define the legitimacy of predictive telematics more than technology itself. Drivers will adopt monitoring systems only when they trust that their data serves their interests. Transparent governance transforms predictive telematics from a potential intrusion into a partnership built on shared value. Ethical use of driver data ensures that innovation remains aligned with human dignity and social responsibility, the very principles that sustain the trust at the heart of insurance.

Chapter 7 ROUTE OPTIMIZATION AND INTELLIGENT MOBILITY SYSTEMS

The science of route optimization has transformed how insurers, logistics providers, and fleet operators manage movement, cost, and risk. In the past, route planning relied on human intuition or static maps. Drivers often chose paths based on familiarity rather than efficiency. Today, intelligent mobility systems powered by artificial intelligence, predictive analytics, and telematics have replaced guesswork with precision. They analyze millions of data points in real time to recommend optimal routes, balance fuel consumption, reduce delays, and minimize exposure to hazards. For insurers, route optimization has become a crucial factor in both operational efficiency and risk reduction.

The fundamental idea behind route optimization is simple: find the best possible path between two or more locations under specific conditions. What makes modern systems revolutionary is their ability to account for dozens of dynamic variables simultaneously; traffic density, weather, road construction, vehicle condition, and even driver behavior. Algorithms continuously process this information to adjust routes as conditions change. A delivery truck encountering congestion on a major highway can be rerouted instantly to a safer and faster path. In insurance contexts, such adjustments directly translate to lower claims, fewer accidents, and improved overall safety metrics.

Artificial intelligence enables these systems to go beyond navigation. Predictive models can anticipate high-risk routes based on historical accident data and telematics input. If a road segment has a pattern of sudden braking, collisions, or poor lighting, the system learns to avoid it when calculating future routes. This predictive intelligence not only improves operational efficiency but actively prevents losses. For insurers, this represents a shift from compensating risk to eliminating it before it occurs.

Route optimization also intersects with sustainability. Intelligent mobility systems minimize fuel usage and reduce carbon emissions by eliminating unnecessary idling and optimizing travel sequences. In large fleets, even small improvements per vehicle can lead to substantial cost savings and environmental benefits. Insurers increasingly recognize this as part of broader corporate sustainability goals. Reduced emissions, lower maintenance costs, and fewer accidents create a positive feedback loop that strengthens both profitability and environmental responsibility.

The power of intelligent mobility lies in integration. Route optimization does not function in isolation, it interacts with driver risk scoring, vehicle telematics, and real-time environmental data. The most advanced platforms merge these elements into a single mobility ecosystem. Drivers receive personalized navigation instructions based on their behavioral profiles, vehicles communicate mechanical status directly to maintenance hubs, and insurers monitor fleet performance through unified dashboards. The result is an ecosystem where data drives every decision, and every decision reinforces safety and efficiency.

The future of route optimization extends beyond roads. With the growth of drones, electric vehicles, and autonomous fleets, intelligent mobility will soon span air, sea, and urban delivery networks. Algorithms will coordinate multimodal transport systems where trucks, bikes, and drones collaborate to complete a single logistics chain. Each mode will be assigned routes based on cost, speed, and environmental constraints. Insurance products will evolve alongside these innovations, offering dynamic coverage that adjusts to real-time conditions.

For policymakers, intelligent route optimization offers data-driven governance opportunities. City planners can analyze aggregated data from mobility systems to design safer roads, identify congestion points, and develop targeted interventions. Predictive models can even help determine where future infrastructure investments should be made. In this sense, insurers, logistics providers, and governments become partners in shaping a more efficient and safer transportation future.

Despite its promise, route optimization presents challenges. Data accuracy, network reliability, and algorithmic transparency remain essential. A poorly trained model can miscalculate risk, rerouting vehicles into unsafe areas. Ethical concerns also arise regarding data ownership and surveillance. Drivers must know what information is being tracked and how it contributes to decision-making. As with all AI applications, trust will determine adoption. Transparent policies, regulatory oversight, and open communication are key to maintaining confidence.

In the broader landscape of intelligent mobility, route optimization represents a convergence of efficiency, technology, and human welfare. It is a field where mathematics meets morality, where algorithms serve both profit and protection. The ability to predict and prevent risk through movement design marks a profound transformation in the philosophy of insurance. What once focused on reacting to accidents now revolves around ensuring they never happen. Intelligent mobility turns every mile into a measurable opportunity for safety, efficiency, and innovation.

7.1 AI-Powered Predictive Logistics

The foundation of intelligent mobility is predictive logistics, the application of artificial intelligence to anticipate and coordinate every element of transportation before it occurs. Predictive logistics transforms supply chains from reactive systems into adaptive organisms that sense, analyze, and respond automatically. For insurers, it creates a new landscape of measurable and controllable risk, where every shipment, route, and driver can be monitored with predictive precision.

At the heart of predictive logistics lies the continuous analysis of telematics data. Algorithms track vehicle health, driver behavior, environmental conditions, and traffic patterns to forecast potential disruptions. Instead of responding to breakdowns or delays after they happen, predictive models trigger interventions ahead of time. A truck showing signs of tire wear or engine overheating can be scheduled for maintenance before failure occurs. Similarly, a delivery route likely to experience congestion can be recalculated hours in advance to avoid loss of time and fuel.

The economic value of predictive logistics is substantial. For logistics firms, reduced downtime and improved punctuality translate into higher customer satisfaction and stronger profitability. For insurers, predictive accuracy means fewer claims and lower exposure to liability. Premium structures can even be adjusted dynamically to reflect a client's adherence to safety and optimization protocols. The partnership between insurers and logistics providers thus evolves from transactional to strategic.

Predictive logistics also strengthens risk transparency. Insurers gain access to continuous data streams showing how fleets operate under real conditions. This level of visibility allows for precise risk segmentation and customized policy design. A company that consistently maintains high predictive performance scores can be rewarded with lower premiums or performance-based incentives. The principle is simple: the more predictable the system, the safer and more cost-efficient it becomes.

The broader implication of predictive logistics extends beyond commerce. As global trade becomes increasingly data-driven, the boundaries between transportation, insurance, and financial analytics continue to blur. Predictive systems will form the backbone of future smart cities where goods, vehicles, and infrastructure communicate seamlessly. Insurance will not only protect assets but help orchestrate the flow of global movement itself.

7.2 Autonomous Vehicles and Future Insurance Models

The emergence of autonomous vehicles marks one of the most significant disruptions in the history of mobility and insurance. Self-driving technology, powered by artificial intelligence, computer vision, and real-time telematics, is redefining what it means to drive—and what it means to insure. The shift from human-controlled vehicles to algorithm-controlled systems changes the very foundation of risk. Responsibility moves from individuals to manufacturers, software developers, and network operators.

Autonomous vehicles rely on a combination of sensors, radar, cameras, and AI-driven decision-making to navigate the world. These systems generate immense amounts of data, continuously learning from every kilometer traveled. For insurers, this creates both opportunity and challenge. On one hand, automation promises fewer accidents, reduced human error, and lower claim volumes. On the other, it raises complex legal and ethical questions about liability. When a collision occurs, who is at fault, the owner, the manufacturer, or the algorithm?

To adapt, insurers are beginning to design new coverage models centered on technology rather than drivers. Product liability insurance for software and hardware developers will become as important as traditional motor insurance for consumers. Policies may also evolve into hybrid structures where premiums depend on system performance and algorithm reliability. Instead of evaluating how a person drives, insurers will assess how well an autonomous system predicts and avoids risk.

The arrival of autonomous fleets will further transform commercial insurance. In logistics, fully automated delivery systems will operate 24 hours a day without fatigue or distraction. Telematics and AI will monitor every movement, allowing insurers to calculate risk exposure in real time. Premiums may become usage-based, adjusting dynamically to the amount of time or distance traveled under autonomous control.

Ethical governance will remain critical. Even with automation, complete elimination of accidents is unlikely. Insurers will need transparent frameworks for investigating incidents and attributing accountability among human operators, machine-learning systems, and external factors. Regulatory agencies will play a major role in setting standards for safety data sharing, algorithm testing, and cybersecurity.

Autonomous technology also introduces new risk categories. Cyberattacks, sensor malfunctions, and software corruption can cause severe damage if not properly managed. Future insurance models will therefore include cybersecurity clauses and algorithm audit requirements as part of standard coverage. Insurers who understand both software engineering and behavioral data will be best positioned to manage these emerging risks.

The evolution toward autonomy will ultimately redefine the relationship between mobility, responsibility, and trust. Insurance will no longer exist solely to repair losses after they occur but to guarantee the reliability of intelligent systems that move people and goods safely. In the coming years, route optimization, predictive logistics, and autonomous control will converge into one unified framework, a digital nervous system for global mobility. In this world, insurance becomes more than protection; it becomes the architecture of confidence that keeps motion safe, predictable, and human-centered, even when humans are no longer behind the wheel.

Chapter 8 ACCIDENT FREQUENCY FORECASTING AND RISK PREVENTION SYSTEMS

Accident forecasting has evolved from statistical estimation into a sophisticated discipline powered by artificial intelligence, data integration, and predictive modeling. In traditional insurance, accident frequency was measured retrospectively, based on claims data and historical patterns. While useful, this backward-looking approach failed to capture the speed at which risk environments change. The introduction of telematics, cloud computing, and real-time analytics has replaced probability with precision. Insurers can now forecast accidents before they happen, identify contributing factors, and design systems that prevent them entirely.

Accident frequency forecasting begins with data. Every trip, route, and driver generates an immense stream of information that includes speed variation, braking patterns, weather conditions, road type, and traffic flow. Machine learning models analyze these variables to identify correlations between driving behavior and accident occurrence. By combining millions of such data points, predictive systems can calculate the likelihood of accidents across specific times, locations, or driver categories. These predictions are not abstract, they directly influence insurance pricing, fleet scheduling, and road safety strategies.

The strength of these models lies in their ability to recognize subtle relationships. A pattern of mild fatigue behavior, such as inconsistent lane keeping or delayed reaction times, can predict a high-risk event hours before it happens. When integrated with telematics, these models can send automated alerts to drivers or fleet managers, recommending rest stops, alternate routes, or reduced speeds. What once required post-accident investigation now becomes real-time prevention.

Insurance companies use accident forecasting to manage exposure more effectively. Predictive insights allow them to estimate future claim volumes and set reserves accordingly. This financial preparedness not only stabilizes operations but also supports fairer pricing models. Customers with consistently low-risk profiles benefit from discounts, while high-risk drivers receive coaching or coverage adjustments. Predictive forecasting thus transforms risk management into a dynamic partnership between insurer and insured.

On a broader scale, accident forecasting contributes to public safety. Aggregated data from insurers and telematics providers can help governments identify accident-prone zones, dangerous intersections, or time periods with elevated risk. Authorities can then implement targeted interventions such as speed regulation, improved lighting, or enhanced signage. In this way, predictive insurance data becomes an instrument for social good, bridging private innovation and public policy.

The effectiveness of accident forecasting systems depends on data quality. Incomplete, inconsistent, or biased data can distort predictions. To maintain reliability, insurers must establish rigorous data governance frameworks that include cleansing, validation, and periodic recalibration of models. Machine learning algorithms must be retrained continuously as driving behavior, vehicle technology, and environmental conditions evolve. Stagnant models can become obsolete within months if not updated to reflect current realities.

Technology alone cannot prevent accidents; human cooperation remains essential. Predictive alerts and recommendations must be designed to be intuitive and actionable. Overly frequent or complex notifications can lead to fatigue or neglect. The best systems balance precision with empathy, providing the right message at the right time in a format drivers trust. Behavioral psychology plays a role here, shaping how predictive insights are communicated for maximum impact.

One of the greatest achievements of predictive systems is their ability to personalize prevention. Rather than applying general safety rules to all drivers, algorithms can tailor interventions to individual risk profiles. A driver prone to speeding receives different alerts than one affected by fatigue. Fleet operators can assign training programs specific to each employee's behavioral patterns. This personalization not only improves safety but also enhances engagement, as users feel supported rather than monitored.

Accident forecasting also supports innovation in claims analytics. When an accident does occur, predictive models assist in reconstruction. By comparing telematics data with predictive patterns, systems can determine whether the event aligns with expected causes or represents an anomaly. This speeds up investigations and helps distinguish genuine accidents from fraudulent claims. In effect, forecasting closes the loop between prevention and resolution.

Looking forward, accident prevention systems will become increasingly autonomous. Vehicles equipped with predictive AI will communicate directly with infrastructure, adjusting their behavior in real time. Smart roads will detect hazards and relay alerts to nearby vehicles. Drones and traffic sensors will monitor large transport networks, feeding continuous data into predictive systems that oversee entire regions. The insurance role in this ecosystem will expand from underwriting to orchestration, managing safety networks that operate at national and global scales.

The convergence of forecasting and prevention signifies a philosophical transformation in insurance. The focus shifts from indemnity to anticipation, from compensation to collaboration. Insurers no longer stand outside the chain of events; they become active participants in shaping safer mobility. Every prediction, alert, and intervention is a form of protection; proof that data can save not just money but lives.

Accident frequency forecasting thus represents the most humane form of artificial intelligence: one that learns not to replace humans but to protect them. It observes, anticipates, and guides without judgment. As these systems mature, their purpose will extend beyond risk reduction to societal resilience. A world where accidents can be predicted and prevented is not an abstract dream; it is the logical outcome of intelligence applied with responsibility.

8.1 Data Integration and Model Refinement

Accurate forecasting depends on data integration. No single dataset can explain why accidents happen; it is the combination of behavioral, environmental, and mechanical information that reveals the full picture. Predictive models require continuous inflows from telematics, weather sensors, road infrastructure, and vehicle diagnostics. This integration ensures that each prediction reflects current conditions rather than outdated assumptions.

The refinement process begins with data harmonization. Information gathered from different sources often arrives in inconsistent formats or time intervals. Machine learning pipelines align these variations by standardizing timestamps, units, and variables. Once aligned, the data undergoes cleansing to remove noise and outliers that could distort results. For instance, extreme sensor readings caused by temporary malfunctions must be filtered before training predictive models.

Model refinement follows the same principle of precision. Algorithms must be evaluated against real-world outcomes to verify accuracy. Feedback loops compare predicted accident probabilities with actual incident records, allowing systems to adjust their parameters. Continuous calibration keeps models sensitive to evolving conditions such as changes in traffic regulations or weather patterns. The integration of real-time data further enhances responsiveness, ensuring that forecasts remain reliable across diverse scenarios.

Effective data integration also supports cross-domain innovation. Combining insurance data with public safety and transportation datasets allows for a more comprehensive understanding of national and regional risk trends. Shared insight leads to smarter urban design, improved policy frameworks, and stronger collaboration between private insurers and public institutions.

8.2 Collaborative Ecosystems for Safety Intelligence

The next evolution of accident forecasting lies in collaboration. Predictive safety systems cannot thrive in isolation; they require cooperation among insurers, fleet operators, technology firms, and government agencies. These partnerships create ecosystems where information flows freely yet securely, transforming scattered insights into collective intelligence.

Insurers contribute risk analytics and claim histories, technology companies supply telematics platforms and artificial intelligence models, while public authorities provide infrastructure and regulatory oversight. Together, they form a continuous learning network that strengthens the entire safety value chain. This cooperative approach allows for faster response to emerging risks, such as new driving technologies or environmental disruptions.

Collaborative ecosystems also enable resource sharing. Instead of duplicating efforts, stakeholders can pool data to build universal safety indices that reflect real conditions. A shared accident prediction platform, for example, could alert all participating insurers and logistics companies when regional risks rise. These networks transform competition into co-creation, where protecting lives takes precedence over market boundaries.

Governance within such ecosystems is essential. Data ownership, privacy, and accountability must be clearly defined. Transparent protocols and ethical guidelines ensure that shared intelligence serves the public interest while respecting individual rights. When built on trust and fairness, collaboration amplifies safety far beyond what any single organization can achieve alone.

8.3 Human–Machine Synergy in Preventive Systems

The rise of predictive technology does not eliminate the human element; it redefines it. True prevention emerges from synergy between human judgment and machine intelligence. While algorithms process enormous datasets with speed and consistency, humans provide the intuition, empathy, and ethical discernment that machines cannot replicate. Together, they create a balanced framework for safety management.

Drivers and fleet managers remain the first line of defense. Predictive alerts generated by artificial intelligence must be interpreted and acted upon by people. The design of user interfaces therefore plays a critical role in how effectively humans engage with preventive systems. Alerts that are too frequent or ambiguous can lead to fatigue, while clear and timely notifications encourage trust and compliance. Behavioral research guides this interaction, ensuring that predictive insights translate into real behavioral change.

Human expertise is equally vital in interpreting anomalies that algorithms may misclassify. Weather events, infrastructure failures, or sudden health incidents can produce irregular data patterns that machines might misinterpret as negligence. Trained professionals review such anomalies to ensure fairness and accuracy. This cooperation prevents automation from becoming authoritarian and keeps decision-making anchored in context.

As predictive technologies expand, new professional roles are emerging. Safety analysts, telematics engineers, and data ethics officers are now integral to insurance and logistics organizations. Their responsibility is to manage the intersection between technology and humanity, ensuring that machine predictions lead to human protection.

The ultimate vision for accident forecasting is not to replace people with systems but to create harmony between both. Machines provide foresight; humans provide wisdom. Together, they represent a new kind of intelligence, one capable of transforming data into protection and prediction into prevention.

Chapter 9 GLOBAL INSURANCE OPERATIONS AND CROSS-BORDER DATA MANAGEMENT

Insurance has always been a global enterprise, but in the age of artificial intelligence and cloud analytics, its reach and complexity have expanded dramatically. Modern insurers operate across multiple jurisdictions, managing data that flows between continents in milliseconds. The challenge lies not only in providing consistent service but in ensuring that every byte of information respects the laws, cultures, and security standards of the regions it traverses. Cross-border data management has therefore become a cornerstone of global insurance operations, a delicate balance between opportunity and responsibility.

Globalization allows insurers to diversify their portfolios and mitigate regional risks. By spreading exposure across markets, companies can remain resilient even when local economies fluctuate. However, this international scope introduces a labyrinth of regulatory, technological, and ethical considerations.

Each nation has its own data protection laws, taxation frameworks, and reporting requirements. Insurers must therefore design operations that are both globally integrated and locally compliant.

Cloud technology makes such integration possible. Data centers positioned in strategic regions enable fast access and secure storage, while global networks allow for real-time collaboration across subsidiaries. Yet this convenience comes with challenges. When customer information from one country is stored in another, questions of jurisdiction and data sovereignty arise. Legal frameworks such as the European Union's General Data Protection Regulation, the United States' CCPA, and Nigeria's National Data Protection Regulation define strict rules on how personal information can be transferred and processed internationally. Insurers must navigate these regulations with precision to avoid breaches and preserve trust.

Data localization has emerged as both a regulatory requirement and a strategic advantage. Some governments now mandate that sensitive or financial data be stored within their borders. For global insurers, this has led to the rise of hybrid cloud models; systems that combine centralized analytics with localized data storage. Sensitive information remains within national jurisdictions, while anonymized datasets are aggregated for broader analysis. This structure satisfies compliance while maintaining operational efficiency.

Beyond compliance, cross-border data management shapes competitive advantage. Access to diverse datasets allows global insurers to build richer, more accurate predictive models. Driving patterns in Europe, weather trends in Asia, and financial behavior in Africa can all contribute to comprehensive risk frameworks. When analyzed collectively, this data helps insurers identify emerging global risks such as climate change, supply chain disruptions, and cyber threats. The ability to interpret these interconnected risks distinguishes industry leaders from followers.

The infrastructure supporting these operations must be robust and adaptable. Global insurers rely on redundant data centers, encrypted communication channels, and real-time synchronization tools. Failures in one region should not affect others. Continuous monitoring and automated recovery protocols ensure resilience against outages or cyberattacks. Equally important is the establishment of unified data taxonomies, common definitions, classifications, and metadata standards that allow data from different countries to be compared and combined accurately.

Cultural understanding plays an understated but crucial role in global operations. Data privacy expectations vary across societies. What is considered acceptable in one region may be viewed as intrusive in another. Insurers must not only comply with local regulations but also respect cultural perceptions of fairness, transparency, and consent. A culturally sensitive approach strengthens brand reputation and enhances customer relationships across markets.

Cross-border management also introduces financial and ethical considerations. Currency fluctuations, taxation of digital assets, and differing accounting standards complicate financial reporting. Automated systems help reconcile these differences, but governance oversight remains indispensable. Ethical challenges include ensuring that algorithms trained on global data do not favor or disadvantage specific populations. Fairness testing, localization of predictive models, and periodic human review are essential safeguards.

One of the defining features of global insurance is collaboration through reinsurance. Large insurers transfer portions of their risk portfolios to reinsurance partners located in other regions. This risk-sharing mechanism requires seamless data exchange and standardized documentation. Cloud-based platforms now facilitate these interactions securely, enabling real-time exposure management and automated settlement. The speed and accuracy of data sharing have improved liquidity and transparency within the global insurance market.

Cybersecurity has become a top priority in global data management. The more interconnected insurers become, the more vulnerable they are to coordinated attacks. A breach in one subsidiary can compromise the entire network. To counter this, multinational insurers implement zero-trust architectures that verify every connection, regardless of location or authority level. Encryption, behavioral analytics, and continuous threat detection systems operate around the clock to safeguard information integrity.

Cross-border data management is not merely a technical challenge; it is a governance philosophy. The future of global insurance will depend on how effectively organizations align compliance, culture, and innovation. The ideal model is one where transparency meets efficiency, where customers, regulators, and partners all trust that data moves securely, ethically, and purposefully.

As global operations continue to expand, insurers will evolve from being risk managers to global data custodians. Their success will depend on their ability to harmonize technology and human values, ensuring that intelligence travels across borders without compromising the trust on which the entire industry is built. The power of global insurance lies not just in its reach, but in its integrity, the capacity to turn worldwide complexity into coordinated protection.

9.1 International Compliance Frameworks and Data Governance

Managing insurance operations across multiple jurisdictions requires deep alignment with international compliance frameworks. These frameworks serve as both protection and constraint, shielding consumers while holding organizations accountable for how they collect, process, and share information. For insurers, compliance is no longer an administrative task; it has become a central pillar of strategic management.

The most influential regulation remains the European Union's General Data Protection Regulation, which set a global benchmark for privacy standards. Its principles of consent, purpose limitation, data minimization, and accountability have shaped similar policies around the world. The California Consumer Privacy Act in the United States and the National Data Protection Regulation in Nigeria both reflect the same philosophy: individuals have the right to know and control how their personal data is used.

For multinational insurers, compliance involves more than meeting individual national laws. It requires harmonizing internal policies to ensure uniform data governance across all subsidiaries. This includes standardizing consent forms, encryption methods, retention periods, and data access protocols. Global organizations often adopt a "compliance by design" approach, embedding privacy safeguards directly into their software and workflows rather than treating them as afterthoughts.

Effective governance also depends on traceability. Every data transaction whether it involves claims processing in Lagos or customer analytics in London must be logged, audited, and verifiable. Cloud systems play a vital role in this by automatically generating activity logs that regulators can review. Transparency reduces the risk of non-compliance and strengthens trust with both customers and oversight authorities.

Emerging technologies are beginning to complement regulation with automation. Smart compliance tools powered by machine learning can scan databases for violations, flag unauthorized data transfers, and even recommend corrective actions. By combining technology with governance principles, insurers can ensure both agility and accountability in their global operations.

9.2 Ethical Accountability in Cross-Border Operations

Ethical accountability has become the moral compass of global insurance. In an age where artificial intelligence and automation handle much of the data processing, ethics ensures that human values remain at the center of decision-making. Cross-border operations magnify ethical responsibility because actions in one jurisdiction can have global consequences. The challenge is not only to comply with written laws but to uphold principles of fairness, transparency, and respect.

At its foundation, ethical accountability begins with intention. Insurers must define clearly why data is being collected and how it benefits the individuals or communities involved. Customers should never feel exploited by technology. This ethical clarity fosters goodwill and reinforces the perception of insurers as protectors, not predators.

Cultural sensitivity is equally important. In some countries, data sharing for research is welcomed; in others, it may be viewed as invasive. Ethical governance requires listening to local communities and adapting practices to fit their values. A one-size-fits-all approach to global ethics risks alienating customers or eroding trust. By integrating local consultation and feedback into their data policies, insurers can align innovation with cultural integrity.

Accountability also extends to algorithmic fairness. Predictive models trained on international datasets can unintentionally perpetuate inequalities if not carefully supervised. Insurers must ensure that pricing, claims decisions, and risk assessments remain free from bias. Regular audits, independent ethics reviews, and algorithmic transparency reports should become standard practice.

Finally, ethical accountability is sustained through leadership. Executives must model responsible behavior and make integrity a measurable performance indicator. Ethics cannot remain confined to compliance teams; it must become a shared corporate culture. When leadership values fairness as much as efficiency, the entire organization aligns toward sustainable global impact.

Ethical accountability ensures that technology does not overshadow humanity. It transforms global insurance from a purely commercial network into a community of responsibility, one that honors both the diversity and dignity of the people it serves.

Chapter 10 PROFITABILITY, DECISION INTELLIGENCE, AND THE FUTURE OF SMART INSURANCE

The future of insurance will not be determined solely by who collects the most data but by who understands it best. In an environment where artificial intelligence, telematics, and cloud computing converge, the true competitive advantage lies in decision intelligence, the ability to transform information into action that drives profitability, resilience, and trust. Smart insurance represents this evolution: a system where every decision, from underwriting to claim settlement, is informed by analytics, guided by ethics, and executed with precision.

Profitability in smart insurance no longer depends solely on premiums and investments. It is increasingly linked to efficiency, risk foresight, and customer experience. Digital transformation has redefined the insurance value chain into an interconnected ecosystem where information flows seamlessly across departments, partners, and regions. Predictive analytics determines which products to launch, AI automates repetitive processes, and financial dashboards visualize real-time performance. The integration of these technologies produces leaner operations and faster decision cycles, allowing insurers to adapt quickly to market shifts.

At the core of decision intelligence lies data orchestration. Modern insurers manage thousands of simultaneous data streams; policyholder information, sensor readings, transaction logs, and external market data. These are unified through advanced analytics platforms that interpret correlations and generate insights. Decision intelligence goes beyond prediction; it recommends the best course of action and simulates its potential outcomes. For instance, before adjusting a pricing model, an insurer can test the effect of different premium levels on profitability and retention using predictive simulation. This process transforms leadership from reactive management to anticipatory governance.

Smart insurance also bridges the traditional divide between operational and strategic decisions. In the past, daily tasks such as claim processing were treated separately from long-term planning. With decision intelligence, every operational action contributes to strategic knowledge. Claims data informs product innovation, telematics informs safety initiatives, and customer feedback refines digital engagement models. Profitability emerges not just from reducing losses but from learning continuously from every transaction.

The integration of artificial intelligence into decision-making expands human capacity rather than replacing it. Machines handle scale and complexity, while humans interpret nuance and purpose. In smart insurance, algorithms may calculate the optimal risk portfolio, but executives decide how that portfolio aligns with company values and market ethics. This collaboration creates a model of augmented intelligence where data-driven logic and human judgment coexist productively.

Smart insurance also emphasizes adaptability. Traditional business models relied on long-term predictability, but modern markets change too quickly for rigid structures. Decision intelligence allows insurers to test new products in controlled digital environments before launch. They can forecast how macroeconomic shifts or regulatory changes might affect capital reserves or customer sentiment. By treating adaptability as a measurable asset, insurers transform uncertainty into opportunity.

Profitability in this new era is increasingly experienced-driven. Customers expect more than compensation, they expect personalization, transparency, and proactive protection. Decision intelligence enables this by segmenting users based on behavior and need rather than demographics. Policies become flexible, pricing becomes real-time, and customer interaction becomes predictive. For example, if telematics data shows that a customer consistently drives safely, the system can automatically apply discounts or rewards. When analytics identifies signs of risk, it can send safety tips or product recommendations instantly. This dynamic interaction fosters loyalty and positions insurance as a service, not a transaction.

Ethical design will remain fundamental to future profitability. Trust is the most valuable currency in digital insurance. Decision intelligence systems must therefore be auditable, interpretable, and fair. Insurers that prioritize algorithmic transparency will attract more customers than those who rely solely on automation. Ethical profitability aligns innovation with accountability, ensuring that technological progress strengthens rather than erodes consumer confidence.

The convergence of finance and technology is also changing how success is measured. Instead of quarterly profit reports, decision intelligence uses continuous financial analytics that reflect real-time performance. Predictive dashboards forecast profitability under different scenarios, while risk-adjusted return metrics guide strategic capital allocation. By combining financial data with behavioral analytics, insurers can see how customer satisfaction, claim efficiency, and risk prevention interact to influence long-term growth. This holistic approach redefines profit as sustainable value creation.

The role of leadership in this transformation cannot be overstated. Future executives will act as interpreters between data and purpose. They must understand algorithms deeply enough to challenge their assumptions while keeping human impact at the forefront of decision-making. Visionary leaders will cultivate organizations that treat intelligence as a shared asset rather than a technical department. Collaboration between actuaries, data scientists, engineers, and policy designers will become the hallmark of successful smart insurers.

Looking ahead, decision intelligence will expand beyond individual companies to encompass entire ecosystems. Insurers, governments, and technology firms will share predictive platforms to monitor societal risks such as climate change, pandemics, and cybersecurity threats. These collaborations will allow for faster collective responses to crises and better global resilience. In this vision, smart insurance evolves into a form of societal infrastructure, a network that uses data not only to predict loss but to safeguard stability.

The future of smart insurance is therefore both technological and philosophical. It redefines profit as the result of informed choices and responsible innovation. Decision intelligence empowers organizations to act with foresight and humanity, using algorithms as tools of service rather than instruments of control. The true measure of success will not be how efficiently insurers process claims but how intelligently they prevent them. When technology, finance, and ethics converge under the banner of decision intelligence, insurance becomes not just a business model but a force for sustainable progress in an uncertain world.

10.1 Algorithmic Foresight and Predictive Profitability

In the digital era, foresight is no longer an abstract vision, it is a measurable capability. Algorithmic foresight defines the new edge of competitiveness in smart insurance. By combining historical data, behavioral analytics, and external indicators such as economic trends or climate events, predictive models can project the direction of profitability before market forces become visible. This allows insurers to anticipate, rather than merely adapt to, change.

Predictive profitability is achieved when an organization can simulate multiple outcomes of its strategic decisions. Artificial intelligence allows insurers to test the financial impact of product innovations, premium adjustments, or policy renewals within virtual environments. Instead of relying on intuition or delayed performance metrics, companies can evaluate profitability in advance under realistic conditions. This predictive clarity reduces uncertainty and strengthens resilience against volatility.

The power of foresight lies in integration. Algorithms draw data from every function; claims, underwriting, investments, and customer interactions, to form a unified profitability map. Each decision node becomes part of a self-learning network that adjusts automatically as new data arrives. This continuous learning ensures that profitability forecasts evolve with real-world conditions rather than relying on static historical averages.

Predictive foresight also reshapes the relationship between risk and opportunity. Traditionally, insurers viewed uncertainty as something to control. Now, with data-driven prediction, uncertainty becomes a space for innovation. Companies can identify profitable niches before competitors, detect early signals of market shifts, and allocate capital to ventures most likely to thrive. Profitability becomes less about reaction and more about intelligent anticipation, a hallmark of the next generation of insurance leadership.

10.2 Human Governance in AI-Driven Decision Systems

As algorithms grow more autonomous, governance becomes the moral and operational foundation of smart insurance. Artificial intelligence can calculate outcomes, but only humans can define purpose. Governance ensures that every automated decision aligns with ethical standards, organizational strategy, and societal expectations. It is the bridge that connects machine logic with human responsibility.

Human governance begins with clarity of intent. Every AI-driven system must have a defined scope, what it can decide, what it cannot, and when human oversight is mandatory. Decision thresholds must be established so that high-impact choices always involve human review. This prevents the delegation of moral accountability to machines while preserving efficiency.

Transparency is another key element. AI systems must remain explainable so that decision-makers understand how and why specific outcomes were generated. When algorithms recommend premium adjustments, claims approvals, or fraud flags, their reasoning should be traceable. This transparency protects both the organization and the customer, ensuring fairness and regulatory compliance.

Governance also extends to education. Leaders and employees must be trained to interpret and question machine outputs critically. Blind trust in automation can lead to systemic errors. A culture of analytical literacy empowers teams to collaborate effectively with AI while maintaining independent judgment.

At a strategic level, human governance redefines corporate ethics. Insurers that embrace transparency and accountability will attract greater trust from regulators, investors, and clients. The integration of governance into decision intelligence transforms insurance from a pure financial enterprise into a system of shared responsibility.

Ultimately, governance ensures that technology remains human-centered. Machines may enhance foresight, but humans must safeguard wisdom. By combining computational precision with moral insight, insurers can create systems that are not only efficient but principled. In this synthesis lies the true future of smart insurance: a future where data serves humanity, not the other way around.

Reviews

1. Chinedu Okafor – Data Scientist, Lagos

Smart Insurance is a timely and deeply insightful book. As someone who works with machine learning models for risk assessment, I found its explanations both technically solid and practically relevant. What impressed me most was how it connects secure data handling with predictive modeling in a way that makes sense for both engineers and decision-makers.

2. Aisha Ibrahim – Insurance Executive, Abuja

This book could not have come at a better time. The insurance sector in Nigeria and across Africa is on the verge of a digital breakthrough, and Smart Insurance gives us a complete view of how to get there responsibly. The book demonstrates that technology alone does not drive transformation, disciplined implementation and ethical thinking do. I highly recommend it to insurance professionals, regulators, and policymakers.

3. Dr. Tunde Olayemi – Lecturer, Department of Finance, University of Ibadan

Reading Smart Insurance feels like attending a masterclass on the future of financial intelligence. It bridges academic knowledge and industry application with precision and depth. As an educator, I see it as a perfect resource for graduate students in finance, data analytics, or actuarial science. It not only discusses AI and telematics but also connects them to broader issues like economic resilience, inclusion, and innovation.

4. Ngozi Nwosu – Fintech Entrepreneur, Lagos

The most powerful insight in Smart Insurance is that technology should enhance fairness, not replace human judgment. The book captures the essence of innovation in financial systems not as disruption for its own sake, but as a tool for creating safer, more transparent, and more inclusive solutions. As someone who builds fintech products, I appreciate how the author connects AI models with financial analytics and shows how to use data without crossing ethical boundaries.

5. Professor Musa Danladi – Policy Analyst and Adviser, National Insurance Commission (NAICOM)

Few publications have managed to align technology, finance, and regulation as clearly as this one. Smart Insurance offers an exceptional view of how artificial intelligence and cloud-based analytics can transform policy enforcement, fraud detection, and cross-border compliance. It reflects a balanced understanding of both global standards and local realities. I consider this book essential reading for policymakers, compliance officers, and government institutions exploring technology-driven oversight. It not only informs but inspires confidence in what the future of insurance governance can be.

References

Adams, R., & Thompson, M. (2021). *Artificial intelligence in financial risk management: Frameworks for the insurance industry. Journal of Financial Technology,* 14(3), 102–121. https://doi.org/10.1080/25710348.2021.00412

Ajayi, O., & Mensah, K. (2020). *Data governance and privacy regulation in African fintech ecosystems. African Journal of Business and Technology,* 8(2), 88–105.

Banerjee, S., & Gupta, P. (2022). *Telematics and predictive analytics: Redefining driver behavior in global insurance markets. International Journal of Insurtech Research,* 6(4), 45–63.

Brynjolfsson, E., & McAfee, A. (2017). *Machine, platform, crowd: Harnessing our digital future.* New York, NY: W. W. Norton & Company.

Carter, J. (2019). *Cloud compliance and cross-border data regulation in financial services. Information Systems Management,* 36(1), 64–78. https://doi.org/10.1080/10580530.2019.1524332

Chui, M., & Manyika, J. (2020). *The state of AI in 2020.* McKinsey Global Institute Report. Retrieved from https://www.mckinsey.com

European Commission. (2018). *General Data Protection Regulation (GDPR).* Official Journal of the European Union, L119, 1–88.

Fowler, A., & Adeyemi, T. (2021). *AI ethics and accountability in decision automation: A global policy review. Technology Governance Review,* 9(1), 37–55.

Harris, C., & Li, W. (2022). *Predictive modeling in motor insurance: Machine learning applications for claim forecasting. Journal of Risk Analytics,* 5(2), 73–91.

Kim, Y., & Rhee, D. (2021). *Cybersecurity and data integrity in cloud-based insurance systems. Journal of Information Assurance,* 11(3), 112–130.

Olayinka, T., & Williams, D. (2023). *The economics of smart insurance: AI, automation, and customer trust. Global Finance and Innovation Journal,* 7(1), 55–79.

Owolabi, B., & Singh, R. (2022). *Predictive telematics and driver scoring: Applications and ethical implications. Transportation Analytics Review,* 4(2), 95–110.

Purdy, M., & Daugherty, P. (2019). *Human + machine: Reimagining work in the age of AI.* Boston, MA: Harvard Business Review Press.

Schwab, K. (2017). *The fourth industrial revolution.* New York, NY: Crown Business.

World Economic Forum. (2023). Global insurance outlook: Risk intelligence in a connected world. Geneva: WEF Publications.